Praise for

Worthy

"The author's experience is so unique that you just can't stop turning the pages, but it's simultaneously universal. I just kept seeing myself and my emotions in so many of the chapters. I was inspired by her story but also felt seen in my own experiences. This is a riveting exploration of anguish and pain burning brightly into self-respect and resiliency; an inner beast who forges the path ahead of you when all you can see is fog. I loved this book."

~**Elena Joy Thurston**, TEDX speaker, author,
founder and director of the Pride & Joy Foundation

"Chris Davis shares her story of realizing that the life she was living, that she was born into, wasn't her own. In this awakening, Chris was called to unravel everything she'd ever known, everything her community told her she should ever know or desire. In daring to dismantle her life and rebuild it in a way that felt like 'hers,' Chris reaches out to people all over the world who feel lost, broken, misunderstood, or unseen. She gives voice to all that's possible—if you're willing to look past what's fed to you since birth—to challenge the status quo and be your unapologetic self at all costs.

Chris' story is one of painful, astounding bravery. It's filled with hope, possibility, and honest relearning. If you've ever wondered if your life is really for you, read *Worthy*. Because you are, after all, worth it."

~**Heather Vickery**, Transformational Success Coach, Best-Selling Author of *F*ck Fearless*, Podcast Producer and Host of *The Brave Files* and *Was It Chance*.

"*Worthy: The Memoir of an Ex-Mormon Lesbian* is interesting, well written, and illuminating. Chris writes with the kind of detail that brings a story to life, told with humor and honesty, even when it must have been painful to describe some of her experiences.

She shows courage in sharing her memoir, and in the living of her life. Reading this book will particularly impact those who struggle with being accepted for who they are, but anyone will benefit from the introspection and bravery demonstrated by Chris Davis."

~**Debbie Taylor**, Bar Harbor, Maine

"I am blown away by the sheer power and beauty of this book. The depth with which I experienced it, made possible by the masterful way Chris wrote it, was so powerful as to almost evade explanation, making it hard to put into words the way this book made me feel. But I'll certainly do my best.

Chris is an incredibly gifted writer and storyteller. She beautifully weaves happy memories with painful ones to paint a picture of her reality that is tender and heartbreaking and just so real. The story unfolds in such a natural, compelling way that it's engaging, full of wit, and utterly un-put-downable. Her voice unabashedly shines through so authentically all throughout. And, despite the pain of her past, she fills the narrative with hope in a bright future. Chris is a fighter—a beautiful, kind, soul—and I feel so privileged to have been allowed this glimpse into her life. The depth with which the reader is invited to experience her story is just powerful. I laughed and I cried, and I want to do better for future generations of LGBTQIA+ people. The rhetoric that shaped Chris's childhood is maddening and highlights the problems in the system. It's only by listening to stories like Chris's that we can make the future a better, safer, more validating and inclusive space. Thank you, Chris, for sharing your story in such an honest and beautiful way!"

~**Teresa Richards**, Louisville, Kentucky;
Author of young adult fiction

"Where do you turn when religion no longer comforts and guides but instead threatens your well-being, sanity, and very life? In this fiercely honest yet tender memoir, Chris Davis shares her journey about finding the strength to say no to spiritual abuse and discovering along the way the joy of saying yes to self-respect, freedom, and spiritual integrity. Read this book *only if* you're ready to be inspired, challenged, and seen as truly worthy."

~**Marvin Ellison**, seminary professor
and author of *Making Love Just*

"I met Chris Davis in an author lab we both partici-pated in through Publish Your Purpose. I was imme-diately interested in how a person who grew up in the Mormon church would also identify as lesbian. As I heard of Chris' journey, I knew that her story would be one that had to be told. *Worthy: The Memoir of an Ex-Mormon Lesbian* is a beautifully written account of Chris' childhood, adult life in the church, and her coming out. She tells her story with humor, raw authenticity, and a deep respect for her journey. I believe this book is a testimony to God's love for all his beloved children, of which Chris is definitely one."

~**Midge Noble**, Empowerment Coach, Author,
GAY with GOD! Podcast Host

Worthy

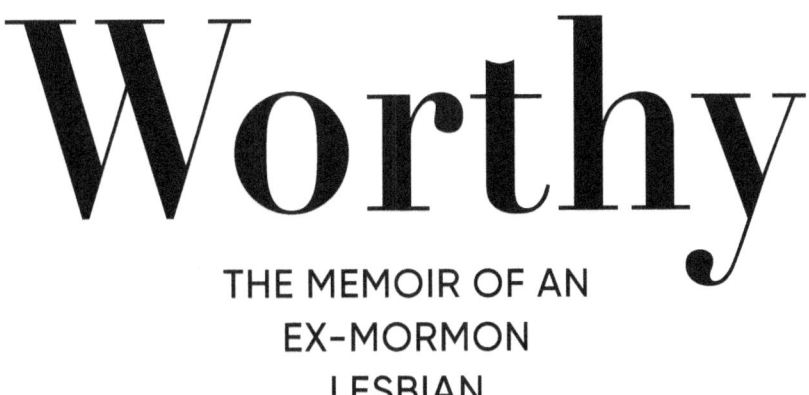

Worthy

THE MEMOIR OF AN EX-MORMON LESBIAN

CHRIS DAVIS

PYP Publish Your Purpose

For permission requests, write to the publisher, addressed "Attention: Permissions Coordinator," at the address below.

Publish Your Purpose
141 Weston Street, #155
Hartford, CT, 06141

The opinions expressed by the Author are not necessarily those held by Publish Your Purpose.

Ordering Information: Quantity sales and special discounts are available on quantity purchases by corporations, associations, and others. For details, contact the publisher at hello@publishyourpurpose.com.

Edited by: Nancy Graham-Tillman
Cover design by: Cornelia Murariu
Typeset by: Medlar Publishing Solutions Pvt Ltd., India

Printed in the United States of America.

ISBN: 979-8-88797-057-8 (hardcover)
ISBN: 979-8-88797-056-1 (paperback)
ISBN: 979-8-88797-058-5 (ebook)

Library of Congress Control Number: 2023906256

First edition, April 2023.

The information contained within this book is strictly for informational purposes. The material may include information, products, or services by third parties. As such, the Author and Publisher do not assume responsibility or liability for any third-party material or opinions. The publisher is not responsible for websites (or their content) that are not owned by the publisher. Readers are advised to do their own due diligence when it comes to making decisions.

Publish Your Purpose is a hybrid publisher of non-fiction books. Our mission is to elevate the voices often excluded from traditional publishing. We intentionally seek out authors and storytellers with diverse backgrounds, life experiences, and unique perspectives to publish books that will make an impact in the world. Do you have a book idea you would like us to consider publishing? Please visit PublishYourPurpose.com for more information.

Dedication

To Christine, who taught me
not only how to dream,
but also how to make
those dreams come true.

And for introducing me
to the dirty chai.

Contents

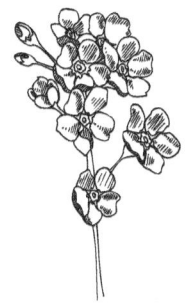

Introduction

From the time I was 12, my church teachers and leaders described my perfect future life to me. They told me that being a wife and mother was the solemn fulfillment of my eternal destiny and that I would find my greatest joy and happiness in those roles. I had a townhouse in the suburbs of Connecticut, and I was a stay-at-home mother. At age 32, I had everything I was told I wanted. Yet here I was in the psych ward, medicated and stripped of my shoelaces, with a husband and two small children at home waiting for my return.

The sadness and depression overpowered me when a catastrophic event happened in my family. From that day forward everything changed. My life's purpose became clouded. I awoke from my sleepy trance of obedience and didn't recognize myself. This was a good life, but it wasn't my life. I revealed my most burdensome secret to a doctor in the hospital: I was gay. I had suspected it since age seven, but I never let myself admit it. There was a puzzle there that I couldn't figure out yet because I didn't have the language to express it or the capability to understand it. There were many close calls over the years when I thought my secret was revealing itself to others, but I kept a tight leash on my feelings and expressions of affection. It wasn't safe to be a lesbian at that time. When I was 13, a man in my town was beaten to death and thrown in the river for being gay. Many of my friends and family members made jokes about the "chuck-a-homo bridge." It was horrifying for a baby gay like me to see how acceptable this violence was in my community.

In addition to societal pressure, the church preached that same-sex attraction was an abomination and that it should be resisted like any other temptation, such as gambling, alcoholism, drug addiction, and pedophilia.

Now in the hospital, with my perfect life awaiting me, I made a plan. After admitting to myself that I was attracted to women, I knew that my heteronormative life was not right for me. However, I had made a commitment to my young family and wanted to honor that. When I was young, my mother used to threaten my brother Stephen and I that if we didn't behave better, she would leave us. Then she started saying her bags were all packed. That turned into her saying that all she had to do was walk out the door, and we would never see her again. I felt that fear of abandonment from an early age and didn't want that for my own young children. Better to raise them to adulthood before leaving their lives forever.

So my plan was to raise our children the best I possibly could for the coming 17 years, and then after the youngest graduated from high school, I would be free to kill myself and finally find peace. Divorce wasn't an option; I was married for eternity and took that vow seriously. Living as an out lesbian wasn't an option; it was a sin—a violation of God's laws. The only choice was to die and hope that in the next life I would be free from this affliction. A fitting plan that would, once and for all, overcome my physical weakness and restore my original spiritual nature of heteronormative behavior and feelings, to be lived out through eternity. Dying would cure me. I was betting my life on it.

The purpose of writing this memoir is to share my experience with losing my faith and finding my hope. Losing my faith in a God who was patriarchal and vindictive, who rewarded sacrifice and punished disobedience, who favored the righteous and withheld blessings from the wicked. And now that I was being honest with myself about being gay, who was I, if not wicked? How would I earn blessings and favor with God with this albatross around my neck? This was an impossible equation to solve.

First, I was a Mormon with a stellar reputation for being righteous and a good example for others to follow. I held positions of leadership in the congregation, in the women's organization, and in the youth group. I received regular compliments on the lessons I taught about gospel topics because of the way I interpreted scripture stories and weaved them into the narrative.

Second, I was a lesbian. After decades of denial, it was finally time to deal with this issue. But just what did "deal" mean? Like a porcupine, my quills had sprung out, and no amount of armor would put them back in again. I could only bide my time until the occasion was right to fulfill my plan.

Third, I had a family! A loving husband and two young, highly dependent children. I had made an eternal commitment to them in the temple of God. How could I fulfill this sacred familial obligation and still be true to myself? The answer was timing. I could be true to my future self by making plans while my current self lived the traditional family life.

So I lay in my hospital bed, planning and calculating the next 17 years of selfless service to my family. I would be a stay-at-home mother. I would be the one to raise my own children. I had kids on purpose and took that duty seriously.

Join me as I reminisce about the nostalgic years of my childhood and some quirky accounts of my family members and dear friends, all of whom I love without measure or judgment. These stories are contrasted with the trauma I experienced at the hands of the church and its leadership. Spoiler alert: I got out!

My sincere hope is that my story will ring true with others who've lost their faith and, in doing so, will help them find their hope and a life worth living.

CHAPTER 1

Cold Baths All My Life

I grew up in a big city in the central eastern part of Maine that's considered a small town by worldly standards. Bangor bustled with a couple of shopping malls, movie theaters, an international airport, and plenty of restaurants and car dealerships. It's the home of Stephen King, and yes, I served him pizza once at Papa Gambino's. My childhood, although not without moments of chaos and confusion, was largely idyllic. My summer days were spent outside riding bikes and playing kickball in bare feet. Yes, I drank from the garden hose. Yes, I sold lemonade. And yes, I rode the rides at the Bangor State Fair every year. My summer nights were balmy, and I often fell asleep to the sounds of the harness racing bugle announcing the beginnings of heats. "And they're off!" All my childhood memories include Stephen, my younger brother.

Stephen was a go-with-the-flow kind of kid. He never complained unless there were onions in his supper. And even then, he demonstrated his protest simply by pushing the onions to the side of his plate and not eating them. Once, as a teen, he was served broccoli at a friend's house. He disliked this vegetable so much that he quickly ate it to get it out of the way. His friend's mother saw that he gobbled it up and, assuming that he enjoyed it, gave him an extra helping. Yes, the accommodating Stephen thanked this mother and ate the extra broccoli. He was so polite that he didn't want to make anyone feel uncomfortable.

Stephen was also a hyperactive kid who had difficulty controlling his impulses. Consequently, he spent a lot of time being grounded. Whenever Mum took away his bike or sent him to his bedroom for punishment, he merely said, "Okay, let me know when I can have it back" or "I'll just play in my room until the time is up." There was no punishment he couldn't wait out. He endured deprivation with grace and dignity, much to my mother's frustration. This was why it struck us as funny when he was asked to complain about something at school and he came out with the confession that he disliked bath time. It seemed so random and insignificant to us, but it was the biggest worry on his mind at school that day.

In elementary school, Stephen brought home a writing assignment about something that made him unhappy, in which he had written the line "cold baths all my life." Mum was shocked to find out that he hated going second at bath time and that her little boy had been suffering because the water was too cold by the time it was his turn to bathe. To this day, when someone complains, Mum and I grin at each other and say, "Cold baths all my life."

Stephen had a peculiar way of waving goodbye when he was little, his arm extended toward you with his fingers hanging down and shifting slowly left and right. It was captured in our Super 8 mm silent home movies the Christmas that Santa brought us a cardboard Mickey Mouse clubhouse. The clubhouse was the perfect combo of the toy and the box it came in, which is so appealing to small children. Stephen's little smiling face peered out the cardboard cutout window into the bright light of the camera as he proudly wore Mickey ears and grinned like a child alive with the joy of receiving gifts on Christmas morning should be. It has become a tradition and an understood acknowledgment of our loved one to salute each other with his wave goodbye every time Mum and I part. It makes us both happy and sad, but mostly grateful for the good memories.

"I would like to wait until I'm 16 to be baptized, so I can make a better decision." When I was nine, I was invited to commit my eternal soul to the church. What nine-year-old can comprehend such a promise? I had no idea what baptism was or what it meant. My father, who wasn't religious himself but was staunchly against Mormonism, had coached me on what to say if I was ever asked this question. He worried that I would lose my freedom and deny myself life's pleasures if I committed myself to this high-demand religion. My parents were recently divorced, and my mother, who was a convert, held full custody, so she decided it was time for me to join her church, regardless of my father's protests.

I rehearsed my answer to the bishop in his office after he popped the magic question, "Do you want to be baptized?" After my statement, he rephrased the question, "But you would like to be baptized at some point when you feel it's right, wouldn't you?"

I answered yes, and he looked relieved. "And you like coming to church, and you feel good here, right?"

"Yes."

A few weeks later, in the cool of November, as we drove in the car on a road that I loved for the canopy the leafy trees made overhead, my mother informed me that we were on our way to my baptism. I felt confused because I knew what I had told the bishop. He knew I wanted to wait. Did he misunderstand me? Did my mother insist anyway? Was this just another thing I was too young to comprehend? I trusted the adults in my life, but I was confused when they contradicted each other.

When we got to the church building, I was told to put on a plain white, starched cotton dress. There were two other girls there for the same reason, and I recognized them from my few children's Sunday school visits. They were a year younger than I was, and they looked nervous too. Spectators sang hymns accompanied by the upright piano, and speakers gave talks that I can only assume were appropriate to the occasion, though I couldn't concentrate on what they were saying. Then the moment came. The faux wood vinyl accordion curtains were pulled back to reveal a baptismal font full of water. There was a soaking tub in the church? The first girl joined her father in the font. No one was alarmed when he said a prayer and dunked her under the water's surface—no one but me! I was mesmerized by the spectacle and had to be asked twice to come forward for my turn.

The tepid tap water soaked my lace-trimmed socks and the hem of my borrowed white dress as I stood on the first step. I saw a man coming down the stairs on the other side, and I recognized him as someone who came to our house occasionally to visit. My dress ballooned as I descended into the tub, and I pushed it down, willing it to stay that way. The man held my wrist and instructed me to plug my nose. Everything went silent for the second or two that I was under the water. When it was over I felt relieved, until one of the official male priesthood witnesses announced that I hadn't been 100 percent immersed and had to repeat the process. Shivering, with my dress stuck to my preadolescent form, I waited for the prayer once again and submitted to the second dunking. All I felt was wet. Cold baths all my life.

This was no miracle. This was a trick. Again, I trusted the adults in my life, but my trust was misplaced. Many times over the years, teachers and leaders informed me that I had to remain faithful to the church because of the obedience I promised at my baptism. I was completely ignorant that I was making an eternal covenant with God, yet I was committed forever to the Church of Jesus Christ of Latter-day Saints.

Last year when I was considering this memory and anticipating writing about it, I asked my mother about the interview I had had with the bishop. I wanted to know whether he told her the speech I had prepared and delivered about wanting to wait. She had no idea what I was talking about. The bishop never told her. Apparently, he took it on himself to approve my baptism without dual parental consent, and even in light of my discomfort with the idea. Even at nine years old I was being groomed by the church. This began my lifelong bewilderment with those in positions of power ignoring my feelings. It was then that I began to realize that I couldn't trust the adults in my life. But there was one adult I could always rely on, and that was my Grammy Sullivan.

CHAPTER 2

Grammy Get Your Gun

Grandmothers are magic. Grammies have the time and energy to do the things that moms can't. I have many memories of doing crafts with my Grammy Sullivan. She showed me how to trace the pattern of a duck on a thin Styrofoam sheet and then cut away the excess with a hot wire tool she picked up at a yard sale. She taught me the power of a nickel at those yard sales in her town. She helped me cut out my "yes" vote from the cereal box and mail it in to tell General Mills that the poor bunny should get his Trix after so many disappointing near misses on the commercials. And she taught me to dress up for shopping trips to the "big town" of Lincoln, Maine, population five thousand.

My Grammy Sullivan, my mother's mother, was a perfect lady on almost all occasions, but she wasn't someone you ever wanted to cross when it came to her family. She defended them fiercely in public and made that loyalty clear to everyone, but in private she offered plenty of advice and kicks in the pants to her family members who weren't making good life choices.

Grammy used to tell me that I was her favorite. I was her first grandchild, and we spent my school vacations together, but I assumed she was saying that to all her grandchildren. After her death during my junior year of high school, my family revealed to me that she had told them all that I was her favorite too. That's when I put the pieces together that every year when she'd ask me what I wanted her to make for me for Christmas she'd make all my cousins some version of that same gift. One of these gifts was a crazy quilt that I treasured for decades. She said whenever I wrapped it around me I was to imagine her giving me a big hug.

Grammy Sullivan told me I could be anything I wanted to be, and I believed her. She said that if she'd been born 20 years earlier she would've been the biggest women's libber you ever saw. Grammy could hunt, fish, and swear better than any man. About the only thing she couldn't do was write her name in the snow, and if you told her she couldn't, she'd go right outside and prove you wrong! She had an enormous drive to keep her affairs in order and serve her family, and she was compulsive about cleaning and organizing her house. Everything had a place.

For holidays and special occasions we gathered at her house. She baked cakes and pies, making sure to include everyone's favorite treats. I especially loved her rhubarb sauce, but as many times as I tried to like her minced meat pie, I just couldn't develop a fondness for it. She also had a reputation in the community for baking and decorating themed cakes. For my mother's graduation from nursing school, Grammy made a cake in the shape of a hospital bed with a small plastic doll nurse sitting by the bedside. I have home movies of her guiding my brother's eager little finger into the frosting of a panda-shaped cake and letting him taste the sweetness of her love and affection.

Grammy had a practice of storing away the really nice things in her home, to be used at some future time. This seemed like a reasonable habit for someone who grew up in the Great Depression and was used to making do with simple accommodations. It was a shock and an utter heartbreak for her when the home in which she raised her family burned to the ground. She lost everything. As she hid her vinegar-soaking pots and pans from the insurance adjuster, she imparted her wisdom to 10-year-old me: Never put your best pieces away for a better day. Use them every day and enjoy them throughout your life.

When I was taking a home economics class in middle school, Grammy asked me to set the table for supper. I did as my teacher had instructed and only set out the utensils we were planning to use for our meal. She gently corrected me, telling me that when she grew up her family was poor and didn't have enough flatware for everyone, and they'd all share a mason jar of water in the middle of the table. Because of her deprivation, she put everything out at every meal as a kind of daily celebration of abundance.

Another thing my Grammy continues to do for me is remind me of my power. She appears frequently in my mind and heart when I think I can't face a difficult situation. Her influence, though she died when I was in high school, lives and thrives within me. I keep her alive by remembering her words and deeds recalling how much she loved me and believed in me. She would've protected me fiercely had she known the secret I was living with at home. Grammy would never have approved.

Family Prayer
by Chris Davis

Four of us gather
in my preteen bedroom.
We kneel
to thank God.

Thank God
for the plush carpet
under my knees.

Thank God
for the Garfield poster
over my bed.

Thank God
for Grammy's crazy quilt
and its colorful patchwork.

Chris Davis

Thank God
for the princess lamp
on my nightstand
that casts the dim lighting.

Thank God
for a loving family
who prays together.

Dear God,
let this prayer
never end.

Amen.

I pull Grammy's quilt squares up
and tuck them under my armpits
nice and tight
like a shield.

Brother hugs me goodnight
and leaves for his own bedroom.
Mother hugs me goodnight
and wishes me sweet dreams
on her way out the door.

Worthy

Stepfather lingers.
Shadows crawl
out from their hiding places.
Garfield witnesses actions
which are confusing.
I do not like
this attention,
but I assume
I am supposed to
try to enjoy
the assault.

Dear God,
is this what
stepfathers do?

I am the human sacrifice
on the altar
of my squeaky bed frame.
He turns off my lamp
and dims the brightness
of my childhood.
He leaves footprints
in the thick pile
of my carpet
as he exits the scene.

Chris Davis

Amen.

I struggle to fall asleep
with the smell of
my stepfather's breath
on my lips.
I adjust my nightgown
for warmth.
Thank God
the prayer is over.
I will be a peacemaker
and not cause contention
in our home.
I will keep the peace.
I will hold my peace.

My peace is forever shattered.

Amen.

Four of us gather
for family prayer
again the next night.
Thank God
for a loving family
who prays together.

Worthy

Dear God,
let this prayer
never end.

Amen.

Family prayers like these that were happening in my bedroom were an example of not being able to trust the adults in my life. Perhaps it was Grammy's fierce love and support that gave me the courage to speak up eventually. At a sleepover church youth camp one day, three of my friends and I were talking about kissing boys. I knew I had a secret, but I didn't understand that what I was describing to my friends about my stepfather was considered assault. They were shocked and speechless. That's when I knew something was terribly wrong.

I went to my church youth group leader Hannah and described the adult experiences I had had as a child only two years earlier. She interrupted me to hold me tight and rocked me to comfort herself. She cried and told me I needed to go to the bishop because he would know what to do.

My bishop, my spiritual adviser, my priesthood leader, my assigned confidant, told me there was nothing he could do. The bishop couldn't help me hold my stepfather accountable because my stepfather had been baptized between the time of the abuse and the time of my reporting it to him. "In the eyes of the church, your stepfather was forgiven of all of his sins and transgressions when he entered the waters of baptism. He is clean and faultless. There is nothing I can do," the bishop explained over steepled fingertips. "It is important for you to move on from this and try not to think of it ever again."

There was no discussion about telling my mother, alerting the police, observing the statute of limitations, getting counseling, or expressions of love, empathy, or peace. He was cold and patriarchal, unbending and not to be disobeyed. His word was final, and I was escorted out of his carpeted office and into the desolate hallway of the church building. I was alone. I wasn't going to get any help. My stepfather had won. In his world of adults at church, I didn't matter. I felt like a hermit crab without a shell—naked, vulnerable, unprotected, scared. Grammy would not have approved. In fact, she probably would've rummaged around in her closet for her rifle and paid my stepfather a visit with an impromptu performance of "Grammy Get Your Gun" to enforce her cold steel diplomacy.

Two years later when I was in high school, my mother and stepfather prepared to go to the temple in Washington, DC, to have their marriage relationship sealed for eternity. This is an essential ordinance in the church for married couples and their children; however, my brother and I were not invited to participate. I tried one last time to alert the church authorities that my stepfather wasn't worthy to enter the temple because of what he had done to me only a few years earlier. I confided in the stake president, the man to whom the bishop reports. I knew my stepfather was required to pass a worthiness interview with him before receiving permission to enter the temple. The stake president was a friend of mine and my early-morning seminary teacher, so I felt comfortable confiding in him and was sure that he would hear me and take action. I wanted my stepfather to be held accountable and answer for his sins before being found worthy. The stake president expressed sympathy and assured me that the matter would be addressed. This gesture brought me some hope and a measure of peace, like an overturned turtle that's been turned upright.

A few weeks later, while I was practicing the piano, my stepfather walked into our living room and mumbled an apology.

"You know what happened before?" he said to the back of my head. "Well, I'm sorry." And then he kept walking through to exit at the other side of the room.

That was it. That was his accountability. Not only was he given the sacred privilege of a temple recommendation, but he was also asked to fill a leadership position in the congregation. It was as if he had come out of this stronger and more powerful than before. I was at a loss. This was the moment I started feeling that victims were silenced in the church and that perpetrators were protected and even rewarded. This was a patriarchal party to which I was not invited.

Another year went by, and I finally got up the courage to tell my mother about the abuse. I felt creepy around my stepfather and was considering opting into foster care. At first she said that I must be mistaken or confused. Then after a pause she said, "You do what you feel like you need to do, Christi, but he is my husband. The day will come when you grow up and move away, and then he'll be the only thing I have left. I am standing by my husband."

This was the moment I started hating her. She made it clear that she would never be my ally, much less my advocate. Once again, I was alone in this world. No one would rescue me. No one would be held accountable. There would be no resolution to my pain and suffering.

It's interesting to note that they were divorced before a decade had passed. He stopped going to church, which was a deal breaker for my mother. They grew apart and separated when I was in my college years. I choose not to have contact with him, and my children know very little about him. Thank God that prayer is over. As Grammy Sullivan taught me, I only wanted to hold onto things of value.

CHAPTER 3

Get the Stink Blowed Off Ya

Grammy Sullivan passed away in February of 1988 after wrestling with cancer. She was a lifelong smoker, and her diagnosis came three years after she quit what she called "a nasty habit." I still have a saltshaker that I gave her in the hospital before she died. A couple of years earlier, Grammy, Mum, and I had gone to a Chinese restaurant. I recall judging Grammy for sprinkling salt on each forkful before putting it in her mouth. I scolded her for over-seasoning and cautioned her about the health problems she could face if she continued. Then I took the shaker away from her and said I wanted her to be around for a long time to come. She frowned. I felt slightly guilty, but my heart was in the right place. After she got sick and had to stay in the hospital, she complained that the food was too bland. Still feeling the pang of guilt for scolding her and taking her salt away, I rushed to the store and brought back a disposable shaker with a ribbon tied to it. I encouraged her to use as much salt as she wanted and to enjoy her meals however she liked. We both cried.

Even though my cousins and I were merely teenagers, we understood the impact Grammy Sullivan's death would have on our extended family. She was our glue, our adhesive, our common denominator. She brought the magic to every holiday and made us all feel like we belonged. Who would step up to fill that role now? No one felt equal to the task.

The one place we could all feel close to Grammy and her memory was at a camp on Lake Molunkus. This Aroostook County getaway in the remote Northern Maine Woods was labeled "Camp Pair A Dice" over the front porch in stenciled letters. Grampy Sullivan built the cabin when our parents were young. They spent every weekend at Molunkus, welcoming guests, cooking meals, water skiing, and generally living the good life out in nature. Grammy and Grampy used to say it was a good place to spend some time outside and "get the stink blowed off ya." When friends came to camp, they were expected to kick off their shoes and be themselves. This may have been a pit stop for many travelers, but there was no mistaking this was Grammy's domain. She infused it with her loving acceptance and welcomed everyone with open arms and an open heart. I always got the impression that I would feel loved and included here, no matter what I did or who I turned out to be. One of my favorite things about this camp was the way Grammy decorated the walls with dozens of wooden plaques about the complexities of marriage, budgeting for beer, and the perils of infidelity:

Ma loved Pa.
Pa loved women.
Ma caught Pa with two in swimmin'.
Here lies Pa.

The summer after her death, two of my cousins and I got the idea that we would go to camp by ourselves for the first time ever. I was preparing for my senior year in high school, and Ellie and Maeve were only a couple of years behind me. We were practically grown up! We missed our Grammy and wanted to feel close to her in that special place.

I called Grampy, "Can Maeve, Ellie, and I have the camp key to go spend the night by ourselves in

Molunkus next weekend? We'll be really careful and take good care of everything."

Grampy never even hesitated. "Sure! That sounds like a fun idea! Come by on your way there, and I'll give you the key and some instructions."

I felt so honored that our grandfather would trust a 17-year-old with the camp and the precious memories stored there.

On our long road trip to the lake, we sang along to the radio, which played all our favorite '80s music: Madonna, Billy Joel, and Bon Jovi! We laughed and joked the whole way, giggling and snorting until we had tears running down our cheeks. My laugh was a rapid-fire giggle, Ellie's was accompanied by bronchitis honks, and Maeve was known for her inappropriately loud guffaws, which erupted at the worst possible moments and infected everyone nearby.

We drove the old bumpy camp road in my first car, a yellow Ford Escort hatchback named Piglet. The overgrown trees and bushes allowed dappled views of the lake as we drove around it on our way to camp. The lake breeze whispered, like someone blowing into a microphone preparing to make an announcement. This first sighting of the lot was delicious and welcoming, just like Grammy's sweet strawberry rhubarb pie.

The first structure we passed as we entered the short driveway was an outhouse that we affectionately called "The Hoo." It was filled with boat oars, ice fishing augers, spider webs, and, of course, a toilet seat guarded by loud buzzing flies. Many late-night runs to The Hoo were thwarted by the paralyzing fear of the dark unknown in the forest. It was common to see tiny bundles of toilet paper directly beside the camp in the morning, as proof that a walk to The Hoo was too perilous at night. Our imaginations were very active, with remembered scenes from slasher movies coupled with the organic night sounds of the Northern Maine Woods.

The second structure we passed in the driveway with the pine needle carpet was the well pump platform. This was the singular source of clean water, which had to be pumped and brought inside in two silver metal pails with rounded handles. I can still hear the "ploink" sound the dipping ladle made as we sank it into the water and drew out what we needed for washing, cooking, and bathing.

Finally, we parked next to the cord of split wood, neatly stacked for use in the camp's wood stove and fireplace. The smell of cedar perfumed the woodsy air. Pine trees shaded the cabin, which was painted light green and was easily recognizable from the far side of the lake. Gentle freshwater waves broke on the dirt and rock-covered shore, promising a profoundly chilly experience to anyone venturing into the water. The swing, which hung between two tall trees right up at the waterfront, had scratchy nylon rope and a grayed wooden plank for a seat. The song of creaking, stretching rope swinging me back and forth over the water, the giggle of happy loons, and the slap of the spring-loaded wooden screen door made up the soundtrack of my summers.

Ellie, Maeve, and I got out of the car, pine sap gluing orange needles to the soles of our Nikes. Before even unpacking, we walked to the end of the pier and gazed down into the clear water that easily showed us its rocks and fish. Then we swiveled our attention back to see the grand manifestation of "Camp Pair A Dice," with its screened-in porch and Adirondack chairs, to say a silent hello to Grammy in our own personal ways.

The shadow of her memory was lugging pails of water into the camp, one in each hand to balance out the weight. She was picking tiny strawberries and bringing them back to camp to serve them with cream and sugar, the cracks in her fingertips stained

with berry juice. She was fishing in the silver unsink-
able rowboat at her special spot on the lake for catch-
ing white perch, directly out in front of the camp and
lined up with the mouth of the stream. She was stok-
ing a fire in the wood stove to heat water for cleaning
dishes and washing hair. She was playing cribbage
at the table with the long, plastic tablecloth—15–2,
15–4—making sure each of her grandchildren understood how to play the game. Yes, she was there. She
would always be there.

I used Grampy's key to open the front door, and
the odor of wood smoke hugged us and offered a welcome greeting. The first thing any visitor noticed
was the huge picnic table in the middle of the great
room. This was an unintended furniture choice for
the camp, but it was decided that it would remain
after the camp was constructed around it and there
wasn't room enough to remove it after the building was complete. No matter, it provided plenty of
seating for meals and game-playing. Two comfortable rocking chairs waited to be occupied in front
of the crumbling stone hearth. Ice skates, fishing
poles, life jackets, and old-fashioned wooden snow-
shoes decorated the rafters. The loft over the bedrooms was protected by cedar beam railings, made

from the materials on the property so many years before, and antlers hung above each of the two curtain-doored bedrooms. The wood paneled walls were decorated with pictures and funny sayings, and the stainless-steel sink drained to some mysterious place I never questioned. The large black wood stove sat cold and sleeping, knowing we didn't dare disturb her. And the corner table that held all the dry food showed evidence that little critters had come in search of a few meals in our absence.

In the afternoon sun, we swam out to the floating dock at the neighbor's empty camp with our razors and Dove soap for a little communal grooming. We shaved the tips of our goosebumps clean and rinsed our legs in the lake. We grilled burgers for supper. Being the oldest, I was in charge of all fire lighting, which included the charcoal briquettes for our hamburger meat, the mantle in the overhead propane light, and the gas burners on the range.

Darkness brought an end to our day. We stayed up as long as we could but finally bargained that we would sleep, fully clothed and sideways, all in the same master bed to keep each other safe from the camping boogeyman. We had seen what happened in those movies when the characters got separated

and, unselfishly, were not about to let the others suffer that same fate. After breakfast, I gave Maeve and
Ellie a lesson on how to drive a stick shift. Kachug.
Kachug. Kachug. The Piglet car lunged and hopped
down the camp road with the three of us in hysterics
from laughing so hard.

We packed up and swept the floor of the camp with
tender loving care, wishing our goodbyes and promises to return soon. On the ride home I was stopped
by a state trooper in the tiny town of Mattawamkeag
for going one mile over the speed limit. The officer
puffed out his chest and his patriarchal authority,
proud that he could intimidate three young women
on the verge of tears. It was a profoundly chilly welcome to his small town. He issued no ticket but let me
off with a warning to slow it down.

We got on I-95 and headed south toward Bangor.
When we entered the offramp on Hogan Road, I saw
smoke coming from under my hood. Trying to remain
as calm as possible in front of my younger cousins,
I pulled over and lifted the hood to inspect the situation. There were flames coming from the engine block!
With Ellie and Maeve still inside the car, I lowered
the hood and mouthed the word FIRE! They mouthed
back, "FIRE?" I thought of the only antidote I knew

for fire and went to my trunk for the jug of water I kept for emergencies. If this wasn't an emergency, I surely didn't know what was. Just then, a kind random gentleman pulled up behind us and offered to help. I explained that I had an engine fire and was about to douse the flames with my water jug.

The nice stranger lifted his eyebrows and raised his voice, "You can't put water on a gas fire! You need to smother it!"

The best object I could find for engine fire smothering was Maeve's pillow. When I asked her for it, she shrunk down into her seat, clung to her precious bedding, and said, "But these are new pillowcases!"

Out of desperation, the man asked for my jug of water and told us to stand way behind the vehicles while he put out the fire. He determined that it was just some spilled oil burning off from the oil change I had just gotten. Phew!

Fortunately, Ellie's mom, my Aunt Debbie, worked at a car dealership nearby, so we drove there and abandoned my car for inspection and any necessary repairs. Aunt Debbie let us borrow her car so I could get us the rest of the way home.

En route to my house, I was almost hit by another car at an intersection with poor visibility. My nerves were shot. I pulled into my driveway and sobbed. I cried because I was scared from the near collision. I cried because I was mourning my grandmother and the future I thought we would have together. I cried because my generation was growing up, and that meant leaving our childhood innocence behind.

There are places in this world, like our family camp, where a person can feel safe, secure, and loved for who they truly are. A place where they can unwind and "get the stink blowed off" them. And then there are places that are no camp paradise, where people aren't accepted for their individuality but punished and buffeted until they conform to the norms and expectations of others.

I sat on a metal folding chair in the small, carpeted room with a crowd of other young women who seemed just like me. Only they were not like me. We all wore our Sunday best dresses and had all styled our hair with curling irons to achieve the perfect feather. Though I smiled with the rest of my peers at church, I didn't fit in. The teacher said so, "God loves the sinner but hates the sin. Homosexuality is a transgression before God and His angels."

My own 12-year-old sexuality was still underdeveloped, but I felt that I was different and that this message was a cautionary tale meant for anyone like me. I had had inklings since the age of seven that I might be different, that I might be attracted to other girls, even though I didn't know what that meant at such a young age. The feminine energy in the room was intoxicating. I became drunk with the scent of baby powder mixed with pubescent perspiration.

The teacher continued her recitation of the church's position on the matter. "Anyone who sins against this doctrine will be punished, first by the local church leadership, but ultimately by the Lord himself. He will assign you to a lesser kingdom in the heavens, and you will never be with your righteous parents and siblings after you die."

This was a profoundly chilly message of exclusion. I felt isolated and lonely in that crowded classroom with the white frosted window, the sterile fluorescent overhead lighting, and the green slate chalkboard illustrating how desolate my eternity would be should I choose to pursue my innate human nature. "You will have no joy. You will have no spiritually affirming experiences. You will be miserable and alone." With promises like that, how could I even consider anything but a traditional suburban heteronormative marriage with children, a mortgage, an SUV, and a pet? The plan was laid out for me, and my compliance was expected.

It used to be that being gay was against the church's teachings. Just the fact of being gay made a person ineligible for blessings and participation in the church. It was a sin, like murder or pedophilia, and one had to change in order to become worthy of God's love. Then it evolved into the idea that being gay was a compulsion, a bad habit that could be overcome, like gambling, pornography, or alcohol. Now it's commonly taught that if you choose to be gay, you can remain in the church and hold positions of service within the congregation, as long as they do not involve young impressionable children; however, you're never permitted to date, fall in love, or create a family. You're destined to be alone your entire life, and that's the only way you can make it back to Heaven to live with God and your family. There's also the idea that queerness can be cured either by therapy, ecclesiastical counseling, or death.

This stark reality promises a profoundly chilly experience to anyone trying to stay in the church despite the unwelcoming message. We must reach out to these marginalized individuals and love them, showing them that they are enough as they are and that who they are is not only acceptable but to be celebrated and lauded. Hurray! You're gay!

How much different would it have been for me to grow up in an open and affirming church where lesbians were welcomed and embraced? I would likely have identified my sexual attraction earlier. I might never have married a man and created a family with him, committing fraud against myself, my family, and my church. I would like to think I would've been more authentic, but as it was, I felt artificial, like a sack of Wonder Bread in a basket full of homemade wheat loaves.

It is my sincere desire in telling my story and sharing my experiences to shine a light on the tragedy of exclusion in our churches, in our families, and in society in general. Children are taking their own lives to escape the flawed and dangerous judgment of the people they love most. Let us dignify our queer heavenly siblings with honor and respect. Let us open our minds and our hearts to their plight. Let us, as the adults in the room, mirror the love and appreciation we wish to receive from our peers and loved ones. Let us foster a Camp Pair A Dice environment where all are welcome to rest from their burdens and get the stink blowed off them, and where all are free to love who they love without fear of rejection or social isolation. Let us create a world where love wins.

CHAPTER 4

To Get the Gum You Have to Plant the Kiss

My Aunt Nola was a tough broad. Whenever our father dropped us off at his sister's house for babysitting, he would turn off the engine of the car, twist his upper body in the driver's seat to look us in the eyes, and say, "If you don't behave well for your aunt, she will rip your face right off!" No more needed to be explained to us. Being naughty meant living out the remainder of our days without a face. Got it.

Aunt Nola also coined this phrase:

Once is funny.
Twice is silly.
Three times is a spanking!

There was no crossing this lady. The penalties were spelled out clearly, though I never actually remember her punishing us. The threat was enough to make us behave ourselves.

Aunt Nola always carried chewing gum in her purse. Gum is irresistible to kids. Moth to flame equals kid to gum. The only obstacle was that, in order to earn a piece, we had to give Aunt Nola a kiss. On the lips! Now, there are some women with hormonal issues that cause hair to grow in places where women don't usually grow hair. Aunt Nola had a big old hairy lip. This presented a monumental dilemma. Even the kids in our neighborhood understood that to get the gum they had to plant the kiss. More often than you might think, we smooched the lips that promised that sweet, peppermint-flavored, individually foil-wrapped chewiness. Our gang had the freshest breath in the tree streets of Bangor, Maine.

She was not all business, though. She played records for us on her huge wooden entertainment cabinet stereo at her apartment. I clearly remember Stephen and I rocking out to "Greased Lightning" from the *Grease* soundtrack, listening carefully for the naughty words, to her wincing chagrin.

Aunt Nola was married to a trucker. Uncle Joe could entertain us with the most amazing tricks with a cigarette! He could twirl it around in his fingers and using only his tongue, he could pop the whole thing inside his mouth and back out again. He was like a baton twirler in a parade, and he had our young imaginations captivated. To this day, whenever anyone in the family sticks a french fry between their loosely closed lips with the "cigarette" dangling lazily down, it's customary to ask, "Who am I?" The expected response is and always will be, "Uncle Joe!"

My Aunt Nola's no-nonsense demeanor rubbed off on me. She taught me not to take any bullshit from others and also the importance of standing up for myself. Even though I was exposed to these lessons from her and Grammy Sullivan early on in life, it took many years for me to internalize their messages and invoke my own personal power because of the disproportionately strong influence the church had on me.

Near the end of my high school years, I visited an oracle from the church to receive a patriarchal blessing, a one-time blessing offered by the local patriarch and recorded on paper for your future reflection and compliance. It's designed to show what your future holds and give guidance on important future life decisions. My patriarch was a member of my congregation, so he knew a lot about my family and me. Following is my patriarchal blessing:

10 May 1988

Sister Christi, by the authority of the Holy Melchizedek Priesthood, and as Patriarch of the Bangor Maine Stake, I lay my hands upon your head and give you your patriarchal blessing that you have requested of me.

Sister Christi, the Lord is mindful that you are here today receiving your patriarchal blessing. He is pleased with the progress you have made since you have become a member. He has watched out for you since the day you were born, and even before when you were in the pre-existent world dwelling in His presence, He was mindful of you.

Christi, your patriarchal blessing will be a guide and comfort to you throughout all the days of your life, and throughout all eternity.

I bless you with knowledge. As you continue to search and study the scriptures you will receive knowledge. As you receive knowledge from the scriptures, I bless you, that you will acquire wisdom. The wisdom you acquire from the scriptures will be a great benefit to you as you go throughout your life. Christi, as you go to the other side of the veil you will take with you the knowledge you acquire here upon the earth, so study the scriptures with a prayerful heart. I bless you that as you ponder and search the scriptures the Holy Ghost will be with you. He will testify to you the truthfulness of the Gospel of Jesus Christ. He will testify to you that the things you learn from the scriptures will be a great benefit to you as you go throughout your earth life here upon the earth, and as you go into the eternities.

Christi, you are from the House of Israel, through the lineage of Ephraim, through Joseph, who was sold into Egypt by his brothers. Christi, this is a great blessing to be from the Tribe of Ephraim. You will receive your blessings through Ephraim, which will be many, for you will acquire many blessings while you are here on the earth.

I bless you, that if you keep your body clean and pure before the Lord at all times, obeying and keeping the commandments of the Lord, that the day will come when a choice son of your Heavenly

Father will take you to the Temple of the Lord of the Most High God, where you will be married for time and all eternity. I bless you, that within this union you will have children.

Christi, remember that when you are in the House of the Lord, that you will take upon yourself covenants. Treasure them, and I bless you, that you will receive blessings beyond measure.

I bless you with the Power of Discernment, that you will know right from wrong. Christi, the Adversary is very strong in the world today. He will tempt you as you go throughout your life. He will try you to the utmost, but I bless you, that you will have the strength within you to rise above him, that he will have no hold upon you but what you will have the strength to overcome.

Christi, you will be given callings in the church. Many wonderful callings will be given to you. I bless you, that, as you receive callings from one of your Heavenly Father's choice servants upon the earth that it is the same as if the Lord Himself were here issuing these callings to you. You will be given positions of leadership. You will work very closely with the youth of the church. You will be a record keeper, a keeper of records. This will be vitally important, for remember, Christi, that we are judged from the records we keep.

Christi, the day will come when your Heavenly Father will call you on a mission. You will be called to serve. I bless you, that while you are on your mission you will have the opportunity to work with your Heavenly Father's choice spirit children. I bless you, that it will be through your testimony, your spirit, your faith, that you will prepare many of your Heavenly Father's children for baptism. What a glorious experience this will be for you to fulfill an honorable mission for the Lord. You will receive blessings from on high. I bless you, that while you are on your mission that the Power of the Holy Ghost will be with you at all times.

Christi, I bless you, that if you pay an honest tithing to the Lord, and your church obligations, that the Windows of Heaven will be opened up and the Treasures of Heaven will be poured down upon you, and as you go throughout your life you will have the things you need to live comfortably.

I bless you, that as you finish your formal education, that you will seek out a higher education. You will have grades and ranks sufficient to go to the college or university of your choice, so work very hard. Go to your Heavenly Father often in prayer when you have problems in school, and I bless you, that the day will come when you acquire an education which will be a great benefit to you. I bless you, that you will be inspired by your Heavenly Father to make a wise and choice decision in the vocation which you should follow. I bless you, that the vocation you choose and follow will bring great joy and happiness in your life. It will be a great benefit as you raise your children in this earth life.

I bless you, with the Power of Discernment, that you will know when the Adversary is around your children, tempting them, and you will be able to counteract and assist your children in overcoming the Adversary. Teach them the Gospel of Jesus Christ. Be very close to your children. Show them a great deal of love and affection. Have compassion for them. Teach them to respect their father and the Priesthood that he will hold. This will bring great joy and happiness into your life.

I bless you, as you raise your children, that within the walls of your home, your spirit will be strong. Your children will draw very close to you, and when they bring their friends home they will feel your spirit and long for it. You will have an opportunity to teach them the Gospel of Jesus Christ. What a great blessing this will be for you, Christi. You will be an instrument in the hands of the Lord, in bringing the Gospel of Jesus Christ to your children's friends. They will respond to your teachings and draw strength from them.

Christi, you have a strong testimony. Bear it often to your brothers and sisters in the gospel, to your friends, your neighbors for, Christi, your testimony is very far reaching. It not only reaches those within the sound of your voice, it reaches those on the other side of the veil. As you bear your testimony, Christi, it is being recorded on the other side. What a wonderful blessing it is to know that your testimony is being recorded on the other side and you are giving those on the other side the strength to go forth in the gospel.

Christi, I bless you, that you will be an instrument in the hands of the Lord, you will work in the community in which you live, that you will be a great influence on those around you. As your children attend school you will have to work with them very closely. You will have to work with their teachers, for your children, Christi, will be taught the things of the world. You will need to discern the things you want them to know from the things that they do not need to know, which will be detrimental to them as they go throughout their lives, so work with them and undo the harm the teachers do to them. As you work in the school system, and in the community in which you live, your influence will be felt by many, all those you come in contact with.

I bless you, as you go throughout your life with the decisions you are required to make, that you will go to your Heavenly Father in prayer. Seek out His counsel, and I bless you, that as you pour out the desires of your heart to your Heavenly Father, reaching out for His spirit, that He will answer your prayers. I bless you, that the counsel that He will give you will be a great help to you in making the decisions that will assist you as you go throughout your life, making the world in which you live a better place to live in.

Christi, remain close to your father, and I bless you, that as you do, the day will come when you will have joy in your heart for him. Work with him, and I bless you, that by the example that you set, being patient with him, that the day will come when he will belong to the Church of Jesus Christ of Latter-day Saints. Remain close to your father. Remain close to your stepfather, and you will have happiness in your life, and great joy. Be close to your mother. Let her feel your spirit, and you feel hers. Go to her often and seek out her counsel, and I bless you, that the counsel that she gives you will be a great benefit to you.

Christi, I bless you with the Spirit of Elijah. As you search out your ancestors who have gone on before you the Lord will be with you. You will be able to find the names which you search for. The day will come when you will be able to go to the Temple of the Lord and do vicarious work for your ancestors who have gone on before you. I bless you with the Spirit of Elijah, for he will be with you when you feel that you have gone to the end of your rope in searching out your ancestors, for he will be with you, and he will steer you in the direction you need to go.

Christi, I seal these blessings upon you by the authority of the Holy Melchizedek Priesthood, and I seal you up to come forth in the morning of the first resurrection where you will be crowned with glory and immortality in the Celestial Degree of Glory and be exalted on high. In the name of Jesus Christ, amen.

I studied this document faithfully during all the years of my church membership, and I referenced it frequently when making big decisions. It was the reason I pursued marriage to a man from the LDS faith, so I could fulfill my destiny to create an eternal family unit. It was how I convinced myself to have children, even though I didn't feel called to motherhood.

The first thing the patriarch said when he finished was, "I hope you like children, 'cause you're gonna have 'em!" At age 17, I had already decided I wouldn't have any children, so this news broke my heart and confused my spirit. This is one of the many times that I practiced ignoring my inner voice in favor of obeying people whom I thought represented God. There were moments of desperation in my young adulthood when I deliberately stood in front of the humming microwave to try to make myself sterile. Honestly, I was confused about whether I even wanted to get married to a man, but here it was in black and white: I would marry a man and have children, a message straight from God.

My patriarchal blessing influenced my decision to enroll in higher education with the initial intention of becoming a teacher. After my very first semester of practical in-classroom experience at age 19, I understood that this wasn't my calling. Yes, I could've powered through the years of education and the certification process, but I struggled with the commandment to work in the school system. The whole reason I volunteered in my children's classrooms was so I could fulfill that part of my blessing, even though I had failed to achieve a formal education to teach in a school.

I also would never have served a mission if my blessing hadn't told me to make that sacrifice, but I was fearful that my absence from the mission field would deprive many of Heavenly Father's choice spirit children from hearing about the gospel. Among missionaries there's a theory that I felt church leaders and supplemental teaching materials—such as the song "I'll Find You, My Friend"—supported: we chose our life's circumstances before we were born; we accepted challenges ahead of time and made promises to help our spiritual brothers and sisters be faithful to God so that we could all return to Heaven together and live happily ever after. As a full-time missionary, I was responsible for maintaining a high level of spiritual connection to the Divine so that I would be led to those I had promised to bring into the fold before we were born and we could return to Heaven together for eternity. So, I would remain a faithful vessel for the Lord to bring my brothers and sisters home, some of whom could potentially become a great influence in the church and a righteous example to the world.

My patriarchal blessing informed my decisions about my family relationships and whether I would remain close to my father, my stepfather, and my mother, all of whom had hurt me deeply and personally in my childhood and adolescence. This blessing forced me to remain in contact with them and subject myself to years of ongoing pain. I believe this is what prevented me from drawing the boundaries that would've provided healing and resolution much earlier in life.

Worthy

I remained faithful in my weekly church attendance and all my religious observances, to the exclusion of friends and family who wanted to celebrate birthdays and graduations on the Sabbath. In high school, I was chosen to sing a selection from Handel's *Messiah* in an octet at a local Protestant church. This was a big honor. I memorized my alto part and attended all the rehearsals, but when the day to perform came, I withdrew and refused to sing, citing my religious convictions about keeping the Sabbath day holy. I left my friends in a lurch in the name of religious piety. In my mind, spending time in a different church was not a wholesome Sunday activity. I hate to admit it, but the true reason for my withdrawal was my nervous dread at the idea of standing at the front of a big church sanctuary with my humble clothing and shy voice.

My blessing influenced all these decisions and many other significant life choices. I was told this blessing was a direct message from God to me alone, and I believed this to my core. In retrospect, all the duties I felt required to perform and all the mental gymnastics I had to practice felt like Uncle Joe's cigarette entertainment. So much show, no substance. In the end, keeping the covenants and obeying the words of the prophets left me feeling empty and depleted because my life's work was founded on busywork and distraction. It was a spiritual sleight of hand to keep me engaged but not thinking and feeling for myself.

One of the saddest times of my young life was the loss of my Grammy Sullivan when I was 17. She wasn't a member of any church or especially spiritual, but I felt a duty to keep my promises with God and the church so that I could be worthy to live with her again in the afterlife. The promised blessing that kept me in the church for so many years was the prospect of being reunited with my favorite grandmother, whom I had just lost three months before this blessing was delivered. I was willing to do anything to be with her again. If this elderly man told me to be faithful so I could see Grammy Sullivan again, then that's exactly what I would do. As I learned from Aunt Nola, to get the gum you had to plant the kiss.

CHAPTER 5

Eat Your Chicken Soup and Pretend Nothing Is Wrong

Some grandmothers are warm and gentle, creative to the extreme, and fantastic cooks who perpetually bake treats for their grandchildren. This wasn't Grammy Butcher's style. Although there were special occasions when she baked date-filled cookies and whipped up a batch of caramel popcorn, for the most part, Grammy Butcher sat. Wearing a housecoat, she sat at the kitchen table next to the window, reading the newspaper, clipping coupons, or rolling her own cigarettes. She wore two patches into the finish of that dark wooden table, one for each elbow, resulting from her right hand holding a mug of beer and her left holding a cigarette with ashes dangling precariously from the burning tip. Smoke chronically drifted into my breathing space, and she got annoyed whenever I sent a strategic sigh of air to redirect it.

Grammy Butcher had a sandy driveway that was great for creating sandcastles and other sculptures using beach toys and plastic utensils. Stephen and I built many racetracks for our matchbox cars and sandy towers that we gave nice, close, barber shop shaves to. However, people regularly tracked sand in through the front door and onto the kitchen floor. All the scuffing and scratching of the sand wore black paths into the vintage linoleum flooring, exposing patches of the underlying newsprint and wooden floorboards. The kitchen smelled like stale cigarettes, body odor, and sirloin steak grease, the walls were yellowed, and there was a constant cloud of smoke in the upper-third of the room that burned my eyes and scratched my throat.

Despite the laxity of her housekeeping, Grammy Butcher insisted that we scrub our hands with Lava soap and hot water when we came inside from playing in the dirt and grass. She also had particular habits about the placement of objects, such as a paper towel that was always folded perfectly into quarters to act as a coaster for her beer mug which caused a circle imprint in the exact middle of the square. And the placement of her ashtray on the left side was strategi-cally set to facilitate ash-catching and butt-crushing.

She was short, under five feet, and I remember jokingly putting my chin on top of her head to prove I was taller. That joke did not go over well.

Her temper was notorious. We knew we were in big trouble when she gave us what the family calls "the Jordan eye." Jordan was her maiden name. This hairy eyeball glare was passed down from her mother. It wasn't until I did some family research in my teens that I came across a sepia-toned photo of Great Grammy Jordan. She had a glass eye, a revelation that gave a whole new spin on the significance of the Jordan eye and made it that much creepier. Her facial expression still gives me the chills. Just like so many members of my father's family, Grammy Butcher didn't have to touch me physically to make me scared; it was all in the strategic threatening technique.

To get us out of her hair, Grammy Butcher was fond of telling us to play outside. In the summers on the Coast of Maine, she frequently sent us out to look for "a soft rock." As you can imagine, this kept my brother and me busy for long periods of time. We scoured that beach, climbing granite boulders and overturning seaweed bouquets. Never did find one. Still looking.

In the winters in her small town of Veazie, Maine, she bundled us up in our snowmobile suits and our hand-knit winter hats and mittens, the latter with the string that ran inside one sleeve and outside the other to connect the set. One snowy afternoon when I was about seven years old, for fun, Stephen and I cleaned off Grampy's big tank of a car, disregarding the dirt that rubbed off with the snow. When the job was complete, we rested by the huge chrome bumper and watched our breath make puffy clouds in the chilly air. Somehow, we discovered that our wet mittens stuck to the cold metal of the bumper. This was a cool trick, and it was only a matter of time before we experimented with our tongues, only to discover that we were permanently attached to the front of Grampy's car and would have to spend the remainder of our lives in Grammy's snowy, sandy driveway. It's difficult to communicate with your brother when your tongue is stuck to a car bumper. Eventually, we understood what had to be done. After counting to three, we ripped ourselves from the sticky metal, leaving tongue skin on the bumper. The pain provided a life lesson that I never needed to repeat in all my years. I still remember the grizzly smile of the sedan's front grill, mocking us for our stupidity.

When we decided to go inside for lunch, Grammy surprised us with hot chicken noodle soup out of a can and buttered saltines arranged artistically on a folded paper towel. After Grammy made us scrub our hands with scratchy soap and hot water, Stephen and I took our seats at the old, dark wooden table. We choked down that soup and those crackers as best as we could because we understood the dickens we would face if we admitted our trauma to Grammy. Rule number one: don't volunteer any information that could attract her rage; keep the status quo, eat your chicken soup, and pretend nothing is wrong.

One thing Grammy did well was play cribbage. When I was nine years old, she decided to indulge my curiosity and taught me how to play the old-fashioned card game. Even as impatient and demanding as she was in everyday interactions, she had infinite patience and long-suffering when it came to teaching me the game of cribbage. She encouraged me to take my time and count my points to make sure I was making a good choice about which cards to throw in the crib and which to keep. 15–2, 15–4; she helped me learn the pegging to keep score. Though she would agree to play cribbage with me almost anytime I asked, she never let me win. The day I finally beat her—years later—I had the pride and satisfaction of knowing I had earned it honestly, a tradition that I carried into my own parenting and game-playing. Thank you, Grammy.

She and I spent other pleasant times together doing things like looking up optical illusions in *Encyclopedia Britannica*, studying the angles and the tricks they played on our vision. Every weekend the *Bangor Daily News* published a Mini Page with word puzzles and picture search games for children. Grammy enjoyed sharing that page with me, and we talked about the kids that were highlighted in the articles on the front. She also used colorful expressions that sometimes made no sense to me. Her favorite was "horse feathers!", meaning nonsense. And when someone burped, she would say, "Scuse the pig, the hog's loose!" I'm still trying to figure that one out.

Grammy Butcher passed away from cancer in the summer between my sophomore and junior years of high school. Sadly, she wasn't missed by many people because of her cantankerous disposition, but I missed her. I still miss her. It wasn't until many years later that I learned the subtle art of intimidation that Grammy Butcher introduced me to, but it certainly came in handy once I decided I had had enough of the misogyny I experienced on my LDS mission to California.

In 1992, Richard G. Scott, one of the apostles of the church, gave a talk called "Healing the Tragic Scars of Abuse." In it, he implied that victims may share in the blame for their own abuse and, therefore, may need to repent for their contribution to it.

> The victim must do all in his or her power to stop the abuse. Most often, the victim is innocent because of being disabled by fear or the power or authority of the offender. At some point in time, however, the Lord may prompt a victim to recognize a degree of responsibility for abuse. Your priesthood leader will help assess your responsibility so that, if needed, it can be addressed. Otherwise the seeds of guilt will remain and sprout into bitter fruit. Yet no matter what degree of responsibility, from absolutely none to increasing consent, the healing power of the atonement

of Jesus Christ can provide a complete cure. Forgiveness can be obtained for all involved in abuse.[1]

The talk was presented to the general church population only weeks before I was to enter the missionary training center to prepare for my 18-month mission. At age 21, I was committed to following everything the church leaders instructed me to do. I was ready to teach the good people of California what God wanted them to do with their lives. However, this talk brought me no comfort or healing. This rhetoric of victim blaming made me feel even worse about myself and the experiences I had with my stepfather. Not only was he free from blame, but now I was indirectly culpable for my own abuse. Yes, I had experienced trauma at the hands of those who were supposed to protect me, but once again I was being reminded to keep my head down and maintain the status quo. Horse feathers! Eat your chicken soup and pretend nothing is wrong.

Part of my preparation for serving a mission was to contribute as much money as I could to the church

---

[1] Richard G. Scott, "Healing the Tragic Scars of Abuse," The Church of Jesus Christ of Latter-day Saints, April 1992, https://www.churchofjesuschrist.org/study/general-conference/1992/04/healing-the-tragic-scars-of-abuse?lang=eng.

to cover mission expenses. After I emptied my savings account, my bishop, who was also my employer, calculated that I hadn't paid enough. I explained that I had spent a small portion of my earnings on missionary clothes and luggage, but he didn't believe that I had exhausted all my resources. So, he counseled me to approach my stepfather and ask him for money, even though he was aware of my history with him. Still, I was obedient to my priesthood leader. Of course my stepfather, who was no longer attending church at that point, refused to support me on my LDS mission. But it was the humiliation of asking him for money that was retraumatizing for an abuse survivor like me.

The guilt and sadness I felt because of Elder Scott's talk were unbearable and sent me into a spiral of self-loathing and renewed feelings of unworthiness. This was especially devastating because of the constant pressure on a missionary to live a life of purity and perfection. Any transgression could make me unworthy of the Holy Ghost's influence, which could lead to my missing souls who were supposed to hear my religious message. I didn't want to deprive anyone of the truth and the potential for eternal salvation. That's a lot of pressure for a volunteer missionary in her early twenties.

"We've been visiting Terri like you asked. We go to her apartment every week to chat, share a positive message, pet her dog, and clean up a little since she can't see," I told the bishop. Terri was a blind elderly woman in a Mormon congregation in Salinas, California. Her bishop had asked my companion and me to visit members of the church in his geographical area and report back to him and his priesthood executive committee about them. I continued my report: "Something happened this week, though, that we're not sure you're aware of. When Terri didn't answer her buzzer, a neighbor informed us she had passed away." I paused to determine whether these men knew this about Terri.

There was awkward silence while the men exchanged sheepish glances, then the bishop burst into laughter he could no longer contain. "You rang a dead woman's doorbell?" he asked, with no pretense of respect for the deceased. The room erupted with levity, as if I had told a joke about a rabbi, a priest, and a Mormon walking into a bar. Before I could process the meaning of this outburst, the bishop asked me about the Dawsons.

I began hesitantly, "The Dawsons are a lovely family. They've welcomed us into their home and we've become friends. Mr. Dawson, as you know, was excommunicated, and now that some time has passed, he's expressed interest in being rebaptized." Privately, I admired Mr. Dawson and his family for their strength and commitment to each other and to God.

It didn't take long for me to recognize that this room of leaders did not share my respect for this family. Winks, elbows, and chuckles took a pleasure cruise around the large oak table, as this Good Ol' Boys Club whispered about the shameful things Mr. Dawson supposedly did to get kicked out of the church. I imagined cigar smoke and swirling brandy snifters accessorizing their gestures. Horse feathers! This was the moment I announced that my companion and I would *not* be returning to this meeting in the future—because we didn't feel comfortable sharing information with the committee.

The bishop threatened, "I'll tell your zone leaders that you're being uncooperative."

This threat, on top of the insensitivity toward his congregants, brought my usual mild manner up to a boil. My anger came through when I met the bishop's eye for a beat before responding, "Those 19-year-old boys don't have any authority over me." I punctuated

my point with a heavy dose of the Jordan eye, both
for good measure and to add to the assertion of feminine authority I was trying to achieve. Again, it was
all in the strategic threatening technique. Thanks,
Grammy Butcher and Aunt Nola.

The room looked like a still life of a 7–10 split at
the bowling alley. Men paused in various positions
of leaning in and out of their chairs. I had their
attention. I exited the room and, true to my word,
never returned.

I was three years older than most of the young men
missionaries he was talking about, boys I feel were
just playing at leadership. I was respectful of their
male-only priesthood authority until they used it as
an excuse to treat me badly. Having been exposed to
misogyny as a girl growing up in Maine, I was accus-
tomed to jokes about female drivers and subtle comments about a woman's place in the world. But until
becoming a missionary in the male-dominated field of
proselyting for the church, I had never experienced
this level of discrimination and forced submission.
Even our mission president, who led the two hun-
dred missionaries in the greater San Jose area—20 of
whom were women—had recently told us how much
he hated having sisters in his mission; he said that

we were "more trouble than we were worth" and that if he had his way, he would send us all home.

Throughout my mission, I encountered many men who seemed to abuse their positions of authority. The stark contrast between how I believed the church was run and the reality of corruption and scrambling for power forced me to look at the organization in a new and undesirable light. My faith was put to the test. I had to decide where I would place my loyalties: in the men I was instructed to obey or in the higher purposes of Heaven. The challenge was to reconcile that these men were called of God and given divine authority to represent Him and do sacred work in His name. How could I separate the men from the God?

Six months into my mission, I collapsed spiritually. I struggled to get out of bed in the morning and would lie awake all night, feeling like I had puzzle pieces bouncing around in my head that I couldn't make fit together. My heart was broken. My mind was broken. My spirit was broken. California was the furthest away from home I had ever been, just about as far as I could go and still be inside the country. I turned to the only person I thought would give me understanding and comfort. I called my mother.

"Mum, I don't think I can do this anymore. I know it's against the rules for me to call you other than on Christmas and Mother's Day, but I really need your help."

"What's wrong, Christi? I'm here for you!" My mother expressed genuine concern and empathy, so I felt safe to let it fly.

"It's all bullshit! It's not like I thought it would be. There's so much wrong with the way things are run here. I want to come home!"

"You've committed to a year and a half. There are people out there only you can reach."

"Mum, I can't do it! It's too hard. My head is all messed up from trying to make it work. I don't want to do this anymore. Can I please come home?"

She begged me to stay. "Christi, you need to do whatever it takes to stay out there on your mission. This is important. If you come home early, you'll regret it for the rest of your life."

My mother had sacrificed so much for me. After the church insisted that I empty my savings account to cover mission expenses, my mother took up the remainder of the cost, which totaled in the thousands of dollars. She regularly wrote me letters of encour- agement and sent packages of my favorite goodies to remind me of home. She had been a rock of support, and all she was asking me to do was endure until the end of my mission. I could do that for her.

My plea to come home early was a challenge for my mother on two fronts. First, I was insulting her church and criticizing the institution in which she had absolute, unwavering faith. Second, it would be extremely embarrassing for our family if I returned home early from my mission. The congregation members would wonder what terrible sin I had committed to get sent home before my time was finished. My mother's social standing with them would suffer. Of course she would love me, but the shame she would face would be a lot for her to handle.

Sadly, I could see her logic. She was right; I had to be brave. I had to show myself and everyone else that I could drive through the pain and difficulty and come out the other side successfully. This was my test. I would not fail my mother or the church.

I recommitted myself to the work of searching for souls to teach and serve. I delved deep into my studies and performed the daily tasks of proselyting and serving with enthusiasm, approaching strangers on the street to ask soul-searching questions and providing simple yet profound answers. I modeled a good example to the other missionaries who might be struggling like me. And I taught myself to sublimate my own desires and aspirations for the church and my family, convincing myself that what I wanted wasn't as important as the success of my community. These mental gymnastics changed me forever. I assimilated into the Borg Collective, to reference *Star Trek*, meaning I adopted a hive mentality. My willingness to think independently was muted. I tied myself in spiritual knots out of survival. I put my head down and followed rule number one: keep the status quo, eat my chicken soup, and pretend nothing is wrong— for the next 12 months.

Upon returning from my missionary service, I resumed my hunt for a husband and the goal that was set for me to start a family. I was on the proper life track for this high-demand religion, and I had reconverted myself at my mother's urging. Marriage was next on my checklist of obedience. Cultivating my cognitive dissonance and choosing to believe things I knew weren't true, I continued to ignore my own desires and passions in favor of conformity. I wrapped it up in a pretty bow with sparkles and rainbows. I became what I idealized, and in doing so developed a self-loathing so deep and penetrating that I had to depend on others to tell me how good I was. They saw my behaviors from the outside looking in, and as long as I looked perfect, I could have a degree of warped happiness and pride in looking like an ideal Mormon wife and mother.

On the outside I looked like my house was in order, but on the inside my floors were sandy, my walls were yellowed, and I stunk like stale cigarettes and yesterday's sirloin dinner. I was working hard to maintain my image, but I wasn't coming by it honestly or earning it authentically. Both of my grandmothers taught me the pride that comes from working hard and surviving difficult circumstances to come out the other side stronger and more confident. I was squandering my opportunities for autonomous growth and progression by living by the church's rules, keeping my head down, eating my chicken soup, and keeping the status quo. Horse feathers!

CHAPTER 6

Joy and Horror

E ssex Street hill was the premier sledding spot for Bangor's children. After a snowstorm, we would congregate on the hill to risk our lives for some wintertime adventure. The first few kids had the duty to break in the powder. As the day progressed and the sun changed position, the downhill trail became hard packed and icy. Ramps that had been intentionally built for even more excitement magnetically drew children in from the top and spit them out in a violent, painful crash down below. I had a metal runner sled, and boy, could that thing fly! I don't remember ever running into anyone else on the hill, but I clearly remember sensing the danger of the situation and descending the slope with the anxiety that I could accidentally sever a limb or puncture a lung with that deadly weapon of a sled.

The worst part about careening down an icy slope on a metal runner sled is the false security you feel about being able to steer. There's a steering mechanism on the front of the sled that implies there's some reasonable ability to change the direction of your trajectory. But anyone who's operated this primitive vehicle knows that once you're committed to a path, there's no way to change it. This is fine as long as you enjoy the ride and everyone remains safe from harm or injury, but the imminent danger of collision and trauma brings both joy and horror to the thrill seeker who dares to embark on this kind of adventure.

After a few successful runs, we'd warm up with hot cocoa from the concession stand. Just cradling the Styrofoam cup brought feeling back into our fingers; however, sipping the chocolate lava drink was more dangerous than flying down the hill. We were certain to earn a burned tongue that couldn't taste anything for hours.

The nostalgia of Essex Street hill sledding brings me both joy and horror as I recall the pleasure and pain associated with it. It was precisely the illusion that I was able to steer my life that brought me joy and perceived fulfillment, but the painful realization that I wasn't in control of my own life sent shocks of horror through my body, mind, and spirit. As a member of the LDS church, I felt controlled in every aspect of my life, as though a giant thumb were reaching all the way from Salt Lake City, pressing down on me and reminding me not to think or act for myself—unless it was approved by the institution.

My church life was certainly controlled by mandatory obedience, at the threat of losing my temple recommend. Under duress, I swore obedience to the principle of obedience itself, promising not to question or doubt any directive that came from church headquarters, and even strict obedience to the local leaders and authorities in my geographical area. "Doubt your doubts" was a popular quote that was widely accepted and taught in the church. I had to swear obedience to the principle of tithing, donating 10 percent of our income to the church plus other charitable obligations within the organization. The church tells you that you want to do it, that it's a privilege to support God's work on Earth, but they curtail your membership benefits if you don't contribute in full. So I was compelled to swear to sacrifice everything I had toward building the kingdom: all of my time, talents, and resources. I swore to give even my own life, if I were asked to do so.

My home life was controlled by the church as well. I had to promise that I would heed the counsel of my husband, but he never had to promise to listen to my advice or input. It was common practice for the local leaders to consult with my husband before extending an assignment to me in the congregation. To his credit, he never abused these privileges. He took his stewardship as the patriarch over our family seriously and did his very best to provide well for us. It was my assignment, as a wife and mother, to care for our children and attend to household duties and responsibilities. I was a stay-at-home parent for over 20 years, raising our two beautiful children to adulthood.

My social life was controlled by the church because I had to agree not to associate or sympathize with any individual or group whose teachings or principles were against the church's doctrines or policies. This pretty much left me with only Mormons for friends. It was more convenient to have my friends within the church because we didn't drink alcohol, do drugs, meet for coffee, smoke cigarettes, or watch R-rated movies, and we simply didn't have to explain ourselves to each other. We had a very insular community in which we would watch each other's children, get together for scrapbooking playdates, and share holiday meals together, because in New England almost all of us were very far away from our extended families. A recruiter for IBM, who was a member of the church, recruited heavily out of Brigham Young University and advised us to move to Danbury, Connecticut, so we would all be in the same congregation. At the height of this eastward migration of BYU graduates, there were a dozen newly married couples at church with us, filling the pews every Sunday and making up the majority of our social life. Church was our home away from home.

My financial life was also controlled by the church. As the primary caregiver of my children, I didn't finish school, have a career, build my resume, or advance in the professional world in any way. As a result, I was completely dependent on my husband for financial support and health insurance. Some women in the church are able to balance employment with their home responsibilities, but I was not. My Rachel Ray talents, Martha Stewart abilities, and Roseanne Arnold energy levels were completely used up at home, and I had nothing left to perform in a work environment outside of the house.

I'm reluctant to say that I regret the control under which I was placed. But at the time, it provided structure and meaning in a life that was otherwise noncommittal and confusing. My childhood home life was chaotic. I was socially nervous and shy. I needed guidance, and the church was ready and waiting to guide my young heart and mind. The church provided answers to all of life's difficult questions.

Q: *Who am I?*
A: *I am a child of God.*
Q: *Where did I come from?*
A: *My spirit existed before I was born, and I lived with my fellow spiritual brothers and sisters in the presence of God.*
Q: *Where am I going after this life is over?*
A: *I will be sent to a spirit world where I will continue to teach other deceased people about God and His plan. Then I will be resurrected, judged, and assigned to a degree of glory in Heaven.*

The answers gave me comfort and courage, even though the doctrine was fabricated, but I willingly believed and followed. I clung to it desperately. I operated under the false belief that I was choosing this path, steering my sled. These rote answers were my truth and inspiration and my source of peace and love, which ironically brought me neither peace nor love in the long run.

There's a practice in many churches to bear testimony of truth and share personal spiritual experiences. Time is set aside each month for members of the LDS church to stand up in front of the congregation and give their testimonies. The principle they practice is to say the right words in support of the doctrine, the policies, and the leadership, so the Holy Spirit can speak to the hearts of everyone in attendance and testify that what's being said is pure truth. Unfortunately, this sentimentality can be duplicated by sharing heartwarming stories that inspire tears and joyful feelings. This felt like an emotionally manipulative tactic, and we unwittingly "tricked" each other every month, through tears and smiles, to continue believing and serving in the church.

So what's the harm in believing something that may not be true? Well, as on Essex Street hill, even if there was danger, it was all in good fun. Consenting adults have the liberty in our nation to pursue whatever form of faith or spirituality brings them the greatest comfort and peace. The harm comes when principles are taught that damage the spirits and the psyches of individuals who don't fit into the classic mold of cisgender straight white male. Everyone else is an outsider, trying to make the gospel apply to themselves and disappointingly falling short of that perfect standard repeatedly.

The premise that the doctrines of the church apply perfectly well for a segment of the population doesn't address the fact that they don't work for everyone. Collateral damage in religious context, if it's regarded at all, is regularly dismissed as marginal and practically nonexistent. Well-meaning missionaries magnetically draw people in from the top, promising happiness, joy, and peace, and then the church seems to spit them out in a violent, painful crash down below when those promises morph into something different and demanding. Instead of finding fellowship, they sometimes find judgmental members and leaders "tsking" at them. Instead of being protected and cared for, some may find hopeless abandonment and shame because of their perceived shortcomings. In my experience, members of the church were taught that all men are allowed the same privilege that they claim for themselves: to worship how, where, and what they may. Yet they consistently claimed that their blessings had been granted from on high for their adherence to the church's rules. In the next breath they expressed sorrow for the worldly population who doesn't worship like they do and therefore lose their blessings of heavenly protection and their privileges of temple access for their ignorant disobedience. This elitism that I witnessed and experienced is generally not a welcoming platform for new members or those who struggle.

There's a story in the Book of Mormon about a group of people called the Zoramites who made a show of praying on a special stand called a Rameumptom, made to accommodate only one person at a time. The memorized prayer they recited thanked God for making them elite in His eyes and blessed above everyone else in the land. I fear that I've witnessed proverbial Rameumptom expressions of self-aggrandizement from members and leaders of the church who claim the gospel as preached in the LDS church provides one-stop-shopping for all parishioners. There are devotees who insist if the church doesn't work for you, you're not doing it right. They experience the thrill of joy that comes from living and worshipping with like-minded people when everyone agrees and echoes back to one another how wonderful it is. But the horror experienced by the "others" in their lives who don't fit the model is devastating, and it contributes to feelings of loneliness, unworthiness, and shame.

Jesus focused on leaving the 99 sheep to rescue the one lost one. Where is our compassion for the lost sheep who've been hurt and marginalized? We have an opportunity to save them as they race down the slippery hill, and we can help them avoid the violent, painful crash at the bottom by loving them into the fold and providing a safe place to land.

CHAPTER 7

Krrrr. I Love You, Bud. Krrrr

When Stephen and I were kids, we used to ride our bikes around the neighborhood in our youthful years of delusion and fantasy—before we discovered that life was complicated and play was a waste of time. We pretended we were truck drivers and talked to each other on our imaginary CB radios.

"Krrrrr. Breaker-breaker-one-nine. What's your twenty?"

"Krrrrr. I'm right behind you. Over."

"Krrrrr. That's a big ten-four, good buddy. Krrrrr."

Then we parked our well-loved Huffy bikes and laid down on our backs like mechanics to work on them with our improvised tools of sticks from ice pops and interesting rocks. Never underestimate the power of a maple leaf to help you polish your bicycle to a fine sheen. My pink bike had a picture of a princess on the banana seat. This was an attribute that I hated but my mother adored, and since she was the adult with the money, princess seat it was. I was jealous of my little brother's superhero paint job and the lightning and stars that decorated it. We fitted playing cards into the spokes of our bikes with Mum's clothespins to make that *click-click-click-click* sound that all the other kids envied (we hoped she would never realize that her cribbage deck was missing the jack of spades and the seven of diamonds). The orange rust spots on the crossbar contrasted with the white and silver tassels, which trailed out straight when I pedaled my power princess mobile up to top speed.

Every once in a while, we found a few coins and made the trek to Walter Street where the penny candy store was. Ruby's was located at the very bottom of a treacherous hill. Only the bravest could ride down it without using brakes, and I once saw Mick Jackson fly down that hill without holding the handlebars! His attempt was executed with some pain and a little road rash, but he had my respect, for sure. I played it safe on Walter Street hill, but I always found pride in the accomplishment of reaching the bottom without hurting myself.

Worthy

The store was located in the middle of a residential neighborhood. It looked like any other colonial house on the block except for the wooden sign above the front door, which announced the store's owner as well as the business's name. Opening the chiming front door of Ruby's was like entering the portal of a juvenile pleasure palace. The worn wooden floorboards creaked under our collective weight, and the smell of lemon furniture polish assaulted our sinuses as we moved through the front room storefront. The establishment's mascot parrot whistled, chirped, and flapped restlessly in her cage in the corner of the dimly lit space. Ruby's carried every kind of candy you could think of: candy dots that stuck to paper in colorful rows, tiny wax bottle shapes with sweet juice inside, and pixie straws filled with sour powder. But my favorite item to get from Ruby's was a roll of caps! I didn't own a cap gun, but I had just as much fun using a rock to fire off each explosive circle, ignoring the powder burns on my fingers and the lingering odor of sulfur. Stephen's favorite treat was root beer barrels. Even as an adult, he always had a couple in his pocket. When I was 21 and getting ready to leave for my mission to California, Stephen slipped a root beer barrel into my coat pocket, and I kept it there for the entire length of my mission to remind me to be kind, to share what I had, and to be unselfish. I'm very happy that we were close in our adult lives, but things were rocky between us as children.

Stephen's life wasn't easy; he had a bully for a big sister. We regularly shouted, "I hate you!" and called each other names. We fought every day over things like who got the biggest piece of dessert, who got to climb the apple tree first, and who got to choose the TV channel. His slight frame was no match for my big-boned aggression. And I wince when I recall all the many times I pounded him down, forcing him to submit to my will and whim.

As young adults, we lived far from each other. We exchanged a few emails, and he reminded me that I used to beat the tar out of him when we were kids. I took this as an invitation to resolve the hurt I had caused all those years ago and chose to make a joke. "You better behave yourself, or I'll come up there and do it again!" We both knew I couldn't take him anymore, not since adolescence when he fought back and I realized I was outmatched. But it was healing to admit both that it had happened and that it would never occur again. We were able to smile away the pain and guilt of the old days and move ahead as siblings who loved and cherished one another.

Mum always said, "They may be trying to kill each other now, but when they grow up, they will discover that they love each other." I'm happy to admit Mum was right.

Krrrrr. I love you, Bud. Krrrrr.

Much of my time in the hospital was spent thinking about Stephen. The nurses told me to sit in the day room. I didn't mind being in a room with other people, but that damn TV was on all the time. I didn't want to watch TV or do puzzles. I preferred to be in my own private bedroom with a pillow over my head, shutting out the world and all the pain associated with it. I was 32 years old and had a birthday coming up, which was more than I could say for my brother. He died in a house fire at age 30, not even two months earlier. My heart was heavy.

Krrrr. I miss you, Bud. Krrrr.

He left a 125-pound hole in my 11-ounce heart. I lost my ability to take care of myself and my new little family. My husband and two young children were at home awaiting my return, and I didn't know whether I would ever be able to go back to them. My brains were scrambled. My doctor, who had a body odor situation, diagnosed me with depression and anxiety and assigned medication to help.

I had been taught at church that as long as I was faithful and obedient, I was making deposits into my spiritual bank account. I was under the impression that I was storing up spiritual blessings for when I really needed them. Then the time came that the bottom fell out of my life and I needed to make a withdrawal, but to my utter shock and disappointment, my spiritual bank account was empty. Hadn't I studied my scriptures diligently, offered fervent prayers, served faithfully in the temple, and dedicated my life to service in the church? I pleaded with God for help and understanding after Stephen's death, but I was met with heavenly silence. There was no comfort, no healing, no soft place to land. My disappointment changed from sadness at the unexpected distance from my source of solace to anger at God and the church leaders who I felt had misled me. I experienced a crisis of faith like the one I had on my mission a decade earlier. The things I had been promised were not true. I had been let down again in my hour of need, and this time it landed me in the hospital. The shock of Stephen's death was the biggest reason for my hospitalization, but there's more to this story.

I had been unofficially dating my best friend for the past few months. We enjoyed social outings, like a trip to the symphony, an occasional hike, or a mani-pedi in front of her fireplace on a Saturday night. She didn't know. My husband didn't know. But I knew. I knew I was a lesbian. I knew I was attracted to this friend, as certainly as I knew that Maine would have one last snowstorm in April every year. I could've sworn she was sending out queer vibes. My gaydar was tingling, but when I came out to her she was shocked and shook her head in disbelief. She was interested in continuing our friendship, but I couldn't be around her without wanting more. She was my first love, even though I had been married for seven years, and she broke my heart simply because she couldn't reciprocate. I could now see I had made a mess of my life and the lives of my family members by marrying a man and bearing our children.

There was no place for a queer person within the structure of a family, according to LDS church doctrine and policy. The contemporary wisdom in the

'90s was to get married anyway and things would work out for the best. I trusted that my impulses and desires would become correct and appropriate after marriage and that I would live happily ever after in a heteronormative family. Back in the '80s, just being gay was a sin, like murder or pedophilia. Then it came to be called same-sex attraction, and it was considered more of a temptation or addiction, like alcoholism, gambling, or an obsession with pornography. Now the church teaches that being gay is not necessarily a sin but that acting on one's attraction to the same sex makes the person a sinner. And God loves the sinner but hates the sin. The common thread throughout all these policies was that death would cure a person of same-sex attraction. There will be no gay people in the afterlife, and my reward for remaining faithful, never falling in love, never having a family, never being connected to another person in a loving, supportive relationship was that I would be paired with a member of the opposite sex in Heaven, possibly as a plural wife. This was what made suicide look so appealing; I believed that dying would cure me.

Here I was in the psychiatric hospital, struggling with both my brother's death and my own sexual identity, wondering why I was bothering to live when dying could bring me peace. But I was a mother. If I died now, my children would never have peace. I would ruin their lives. I would create a tear in their hearts that would never heal. So I formulated my plan: I would remain silent about my orientation and continue in my marriage for now. I would raise these innocent children to adulthood, and after the youngest graduated from high school I would be free to kill myself. With only 17 years to go, I could endure to the end. I could bear this burden tacitly without disrupting the idyllic upbringing of our children. I would make sure they experienced the classic simple pleasures of childhood that Stephen and I enjoyed.

I still have that root beer barrel packed away somewhere in my boxes of memories. And although my own children bickered much of the time, I took comfort in my mother's promise that one day they would draw close to each other and be friends.

Krrrr. I just wanted them to know the love we shared, Bud. Krrrr.

CHAPTER 8

A Fight of Black Belt Proportions

Stephen and I started karate classes together in 1980 when we were seven and nine years old. Our sensei, Sandy Holbrook, was a mild-mannered hippie who insisted on strict adherence to tradition. He instilled in us a respect for the martial arts, which developed into a respect for all things alive and beautiful. I found the exactness and discipline required for karate very satisfying, and I quickly discovered that I had a natural aptitude for the fighting arts.

Stephen and I passed our first test and earned our white belt rank together. At our second test months later, Stephen was granted his yellow belt, but I was surprised to be awarded an orange belt. After the test, I went to Sandy and explained that there had been a mistake. Saying there was no mistake, he told me I had earned the privilege of skipping my yellow belt by my performance and dedication. This encouragement spurred me on in class, but it was only a matter of weeks until Stephen stopped attending because he didn't want to be compared to me. After all, who wants to be reminded that your sister is better at fighting than you are?

I continued to study under Sandy for years. I remember my red belt test, which was the seventh of nine belts. The strenuous test was hours long, and I exerted my 12-year-old body beyond what I thought I was capable of. Sandy gave his subtle, understated approval when he awarded me my new rank. I knew I had done well. And I knew that he knew it, too.

Six months later, there was another regularly scheduled belt test, but I wasn't invited to test because I hadn't learned enough to advance yet. I reminded my sensei that I wanted to learn more and make more progress, and he promised he would teach me what I needed to know. One year after my red belt test, I was again not invited to test, so I took my concerns to Sandy privately. I asked whether I had performed at a high enough level at my last test or if I had some making up to do to earn the instruction I needed for continued rank advancement. All he said was that I was exactly where I was supposed to be.

As the weeks passed and I still wasn't being taught what I needed to know to progress, I began to understand that I had hit a glass ceiling. I was the highest-ranking female in the karate school, and I began to observe the subtle social cues of excluding women. Conversations stopped abruptly when a woman approached a group of men joking and laughing. No other women in the school got promoted above my rank, despite their abilities and potential. Sandy's best friend occasionally conducted our classes, and his misogyny was more overt, cementing my discomfort as a young woman in a male-dominated field and perpetuating the Good-Ol'-Boys-Club mentality that was still so rampant in the early to mid-'80s. I came to comprehend that there would be no more advancement for me. My progress was blocked, and I had difficulty not feeling bitter toward my mentor for stunting my growth simply because of my gender. This was one of my first exposures to sexism, which was coupled with messages I received from church about my proper place in the world. Twelve-year-old boys could pass the sacrament emblems to the congregation, but

12-year-old girls were not permitted, simply because they were girls.

School and church activities soon took over my time and attention, and I withdrew from my martial arts home with sadness and regret. I vowed that one day I would return to the practice and complete my goal of attaining a black belt. That dream waited on my shelf for two decades. As soon as I left the hospital after Stephen's death, I enrolled in Taekwondo classes. There's something so clarifying about going through a catastrophic life event that brings a person's priorities into focus. Martial arts was something I was good at, and I needed a confidence boost at this point in my life. I needed to excel and achieve, and there's very little about being a stay-at-home parent that involves achievement, accolades, or recognition.

After my first Taekwondo class, Aaron the instructor asked me about my prior experience. I described my time with Sandy, and he expressed surprise that I hadn't practiced martial arts in nearly 20 years. He said my technique was clean and that he was happy I was joining his class. Having been absent for so many years and beginning at a new school, I fully expected to start at the white belt rank like everyone else. But when Aaron saw my abilities and how quickly I picked up what he taught, he invited me to wear my previously earned red belt to class. I was concerned about how my peers would receive this, and there were some comments made under their breath, but ultimately I earned their respect, and as my conditioning improved, I was able to perform at rank level.

Excelling again at martial arts was a shot in the arm. It didn't take me long to earn my black belt in Taekwondo, but it also didn't take me long to recognize that my instructor was a master in mediocrity. There was none of the insistence of attention to detail that Sandy taught. I grew frustrated with the routine nature of class, repeating the same forms and techniques each time, several days a week, with no focus on improvement or perfection. That's when I began shopping for a new martial arts home and became acquainted with the Chinese art of Kung Fu. This art fascinated me and promised to teach me more than just strict adherence to tradition—it also taught the science behind the movement. I discovered a new curiosity in the arts, as well as a new confidence in the studio.

The dojo was the only place I could be my true self, without reservation. There were no labels of "wife" or "mother." There were no expectations to spread the gospel message or be a good example. I had the freedom to excel without embarrassment and fail without shame. I climbed the ranks of the Kung Fu school from white belt to black without regard for who I was outside the studio. My instructors didn't treat me differently because I was a woman. I was perfectly capable of doing everything the men in the class could do, and in some cases I could do it with greater speed and flexibility because of my size and gender. It always gave me a secret thrill to be underestimated by a male partner and then witness the shock on his face when I kicked his ass.

I was often disappointed by other students' laziness, though. I didn't understand how they could disrespect the art with their sloppy stances and weak techniques. I was friendly to all my fellow practitioners, but I truly treasured my interactions with the men and women who pushed themselves to be better every class and encouraged me to perform at my fullest capacity. It's been my experience that the pursuit of excellence in the dojo is an individual one; however, I found the group setting to be motivating and inspirational. Practicing martial arts deserves a measure of honor for the studio, the instructor, the tradition of the art, and oneself. To dishonor the tradition is to dishonor the history of martial arts and the generations of people who've preserved it.

My sifu, Master Petrov, consistently encouraged me to push harder and develop better technique to make my body and mind stronger. He was a gifted teacher who knew how to motivate and inspire me with his stories and quotes. He regularly asked about my goals and wanted to know how he could support me. Some days I came into the studio and asked him to push me hard and make me into a sweaty mess. He did that. Other days I needed more tenderness and compassion. He did that, too. His compassionate approach taught me to be gentle with myself and accept the parts of myself that might not be on the list of acceptable expectations for a person in my position as a Mormon wife and mother.

Master Petrov's casual, upbeat personality contributed to the relaxed atmosphere of the studio. I remember one time while the class was stretching, he asked us who we thought would win in a battle to the death: a Jedi knight with a lightsaber or a ninja with a poisonous blow dart. At one of the private birthday parties he hosted, the parents forgot to provide a knife to cut the cake, so Master Petrov used a

Chinese broadsword to slice it up with flair into por-
tions. Best birthday ever for that kid! Master Petrov
even held annual water gun fights in the parking lot
for the teens, making sure he had the biggest super-
soaker of them all.

The best thing he did, though, was mentor the
youth in his care, teaching them the importance of
self-control, discipline, and honor. He taught them
how to apply those principles at home, at school, and
on the playground. Master Petrov understood what it
meant to struggle. He overcame many obstacles from
his childhood, having grown up in a rough neighborhood. I'm especially proud of his accomplishment
of improving his physical body into a "lean, mean,
instrument of death," as he would say, after spending
many years in a heavy body that prevented him from
being the best martial artist he could be. The trans-
formation I witnessed in him was inspirational.

Master Petrov's belief in my success ultimately
helped me reach the rank of second-degree black belt,
an accomplishment of which I'm extremely proud. At
my last belt test, I was required to perform a memorized routine in front of the grandmaster, my teacher's
teacher and the owner of the martial arts chain.
This was excruciatingly nerve-racking, and I felt the

pressure of every lesson I successfully learned and every opportunity I foolishly wasted during my training. I bowed to my grandmaster, prepared myself with a long inhale through my nose, and let loose my inner beast of technique, power, and speed. I punched and kicked and blocked. I performed the best routine of my life. I made myself proud, but I had no idea how the grandmaster felt because when I completed my final bow, there was silence. He stared at me while I stood at attention and then called my instructor over to whisper in Master Petrov's ear. Then I was dismissed.

It wasn't until after the completion of the day's testing that my instructor passed along the compliment that the grandmaster had paid both to him and to me: "That was the best form I've ever seen from a student who is not an employee." This was a monumental achievement; one I will treasure into my golden years. I had the respect of my grandmaster, the respect of my instructor, the respect of my peers, and, most importantly, the self-respect that only comes with great accomplishment.

I could stand to hear the rhetoric from church leaders that queer people were sinners and needed to repent of their wickedness, but once you aim that kind of talk at my child, you better be prepared for a fight of black belt proportions.

I turned off the car, but we were still deep in conversation. The garage floodlights illuminated our faces, which showed deep concern and love for one another. My fifteen-year-old child confided in me that they identified as nonbinary transgender. I struggled to understand what this meant—because I was unfamiliar with the complex LGBTQIA+ lexicon. They nervously asked, "Would you still love me if I was trans?"

There was no hesitation in my answer. "Grace, the only appropriate response to your question is yes. I will always love you. Thank you for trusting me with your truth."

"Thanks, Mom, I was worried about how you would react because I know you're so religious and that it could be a conflict for you."

This heartbreak felt like an ax colliding into my chest cavity. I've always wanted my children to feel comfortable coming to me with questions or concerns. To know that raising them in the church contributed to the difficulty of this moment made my heart sink.

I had entertained secret doubts about the truthfulness of the claims of the church, but out of respect for my husband, and to align with the eternal covenants I had made to him and to God, I doubted only in private. Outwardly, I presented as a fully faithful and believing member of the church, to keep peace in my family and encourage and uplift fellow church community members. However, Grace's coming out stirred the mama bear defenses from deep within me. The time to act had arrived.

I knew something like this was coming for a couple of weeks. Grace had been feeling me out and making comments to test my reactions. I was prepared to come out to them to show my support and understanding. "I want you to know that I love and support you," I started. Here was the moment of no return. To show solidarity and, hopefully, express comfort and understanding, I nervously decided to confide in my child that I was also a tacit member of the queer community. "Grace, I would like you to know that I understand your fears about coming out, and I feel safe telling you that I'm a closeted lesbian."

"Really?" They were shocked. This was completely unexpected for them. Our relationship would forever be changed. We connected on a human level, not just in our roles as family members. We embraced and entered the house where we began our secret-keeping from Grace's father and older brother. Grace came out to them within a week, and they were as supportive as they were capable of being. Due to the pressures from established church policies and the gymnastics it took to straddle love for a family member with devotion to the church, this was a difficult time. However, I'm happy to report that love won in this story and that Grace was eventually fully supported by their father and brother despite the obvious religious conflicts.

Grace assured me they would keep my confidence. This was a huge risk, but I was just not prepared for the fallout in my marriage that would accompany my coming out and declaring my own truth.

A couple of weeks later, Grace, then calling themselves Rune, uploaded a video to tell friends and family about their exciting news and explain about their new name and pronouns. A youth leader in our congregation discovered the video and reported it to the local church leadership. The bishop called our family into his office to "manage expectations early." He explained that there was no such thing as nonbinary transgender, expounding that gender was an eternal part of our nature and didn't change or vary from set social norms. He continued, "Grace, because you have come out publicly against a church teaching, you will never be worthy to serve a mission as an official representative of the church. Your worthiness is on the same level as someone who has had multiple sexual partners, so you are no longer eligible to enter the temple of God. In addition, you must use the women's restrooms here at church, and you are only permitted to attend the classes established for females."

Rune was unflappable. I was so impressed with their poise and grace. They had written out questions for the bishop, and he was selecting his words carefully and vowing to get further clarification from his superiors. Essentially, what Rune wanted to know was whether it was possible to be trans and still stay in the church. The bishop offered what he thought was encouragement: "Please be prayerful about your decision. Come back next week and let me know what Heavenly Father says to you about your choice."

We left the bishop's office confused and disappointed, searching for answers and yet afraid to reason things out for ourselves. We had an assignment to pray. That was a measurable task we chose to perform individually, not really discussing the matter further and trusting in the wisdom of our spiritual leader that everything would work out for the best.

The following Sunday we all returned to the bishop's office for another round of lecture and rhetoric. When Rune reported back that they were confident God supported them on this journey, the bishop disagreed. I jumped into the exchange.

"So when you told them to go home and pray about it, what you were really saying was to pray until they agreed with you?"

"No," he retorted defensively, but it was clear to us all that was exactly what he meant. The air in the room shifted, along with my respect for this man's authority. He then warned my husband Gary and me, "You both will need to exercise caution because you will not be worthy of your temple recommends if you believe that nonbinary gender is a real thing or that Grace was born this way." This was a not-so-veiled threat that if we did not follow his counsel and submit to his authority as leader of the congregation and representative of Jesus Christ, he would revoke our permission to enter the holiest place on Earth, which is reserved for only the most dedicated and obedient members of the church.

This message of exclusion could not be from God. There was no compassion in these answers. This was not what Jesus would do. I was furious at the things the bishop said to and about our child, and I worried about long-term spiritual damage.

On our drive home from the meeting that afternoon, Rune and I were alone, and I told them that the church was not true, like Santa Claus. Until that point, I had been respectful of Rune's desire to remain faithful in the church, but suddenly I recognized that presenting my own facade of belief and devotion was detrimental to my loved one. I had to show my cards. I had to expose my disbelief. I had to share my doubts and concerns so Rune could avoid the pain of rejection and wouldn't develop the self-loathing that had eroded my own self-worth throughout the years.

Later in the day, I learned from friends that the bishop was instructing members of the congregation that they were not permitted to call Rune by their new name or proper pronouns. He outed Rune to these people, our peers, without our knowledge or consent. Such a reckless action could potentially have put Rune in danger of discrimination or even physical harm.

"I just don't think I can go back, Gary," I reasoned desperately with my husband. He knew I had been entertaining some serious doubts over the past year. I had dedicated a significant amount of time to studying spirituality from authors of various faith traditions. What he didn't know was that my curiosity had led me to disturbing information about church history and many inconsistencies with doctrine and policies over the years. My religious devotion to the church never recovered from these realizations. I was conflicted to the extreme because I believed that, similar to the martial arts I revered, to dishonor the church and its leaders was to dishonor the tradition of faithfulness that had been passed down from the first pioneers who sacrificed everything they had for the building up of the Kingdom of God on Earth. Now, the actions and words of this bishop were a new low in my church experience and yet another confirmation that this was not where I belonged. This box was too small, and I would not continue to contort myself into a foreign shape to comply with these demands.

I spent my lifetime listening to messages at church about the wickedness of my nature, not only as a gay person but as a human in general. The Book of Mormon clearly says that man in his natural state is unworthy to live with God: "The natural man is an enemy to God" (Mosiah 3:19). How could I let this message that Rune wasn't worthy simply because they existed in a body on the earth sink into my child's heart? This was a message that I would not allow near my loved one. So I texted the bishop with my concerns. After he tried to defend himself three times, I prepared myself with a long inhale through my nose, let loose my inner beast, and typed the words "YOU ARE A PRICK." My thumb hovered over the send button for a long moment before I committed myself to the sentiment and sent it directly to his cellphone screen. This was a significant expression of sedition, an offense for which my good standing in the church could be brought into question. But I was unapologetic, and it felt amazingly healthy to assert my boundary with this patriarchal representative. He didn't respond. My point was made, and I had nothing more to say to him.

My husband and older son remained faithfully devoted to the church and its leaders, which I expected because they didn't have the crumblings in their foundations of faith that I had. It's a difficult thing to walk away from an organization that tells you you're elite and affirms your privilege as a straight white man.

However, Rune and I never returned to church. I broke my eternal commitments and forfeited my place in Heaven, but ultimately I earned the self-respect that only comes with great accomplishment, and I rescued my queer child in the process.

How many young people struggle with the pain of not being accepted for their differences? How many bear the loneliness of not being understood, not because the adults in their lives can't understand, but because they refuse to extend a little understanding and compassion? Hate and hateful expressions will never cure someone from being gay. Familial and societal disapproval of a person's sexual orientation or gender identity may curb open manifestations of these feelings, but they only crush the souls of those who truly struggle with acceptance and belonging. Sometimes even well-intentioned parents will say they love their child "no matter what," not realizing that this turn of phrase is hurtful because it's what they might say if their child had made terrible life choices, such as stealing candy or getting a DUI. And as for me, some of the religious people in my life said that they loved me "even though you're a sinner" and then promised to pray for my soul. This isn't the loving flex they think it is. It hurts.

I can relate with the churchgoers who only want to discourage bad behavior in the hope of saving the people they love. They believe that they mean well and have been taught to preach to their neighbors and be a good example of righteousness and faithfulness. They want others to know of their convictions to follow the prophet and his teachings, uphold the traditions of generations before, and maintain the order that was established by men in authority long ago. Still, I had moments of anger in my transition out of the church—anger at myself for believing that those men who led the church were God's representatives and that I wholeheartedly obeyed and submitted to their counsel. I felt embarrassed by how gullible I had been for so many years. I felt ashamed that I wasted all those years performing busywork for the church instead of pursuing my own ambitions. But with the passage of time, I now celebrate my new freedom to think for myself and experience life on more authentic terms.

Leaving the church meant leaving my community, my friends, and my support system. I had invested all my social capital into the one basket of women at church. I was frightened to reach out to people outside my religion for fear of being led down the road to perdition. Tentatively, I turned to other former members of the church for support, in person and on the internet, and created lasting friendships with many. I reached out to the queer community and was accepted with open arms. I made friends with people who had no idea what Mormons believed, and I discovered that there are some amazing individuals out there who aren't the threat I was taught they would be. It delighted me to discover that they only wanted to love me and share their lives with me. Once I finally dropped my air of spiritual elitism and moral superiority, I started experiencing a new feeling that I can only describe as joining the human race.

I've often wondered whether it was right to disclose my sexual identity to Rune and ask that they keep it a secret from their father. I understand that it was morally ambiguous, but during those three years of secret-keeping, Rune and I grew so much closer and shared so much more of ourselves in our relationship. We encouraged each other. We supported each other. Instead of attending our church meetings, we spent our Sunday mornings at Panera, eating brunch, toasting our mugs of pale coffee and sweet tea, and bearing witness to each other about how happy we were now that we had left the church and come out to one another. Rune taught me to love myself, not *despite* who I was, but precisely *because* of who I was. I had internalized a great deal of homophobia, and Rune helped me overcome it with love and unconditional acceptance. So yes, if I had it to do again, I would absolutely open up my life and my heart to my teenage child who was wise beyond their years and ready to love me as myself. We both benefited from that decision, and I wouldn't take it back.

As I learned from Master Petrov, I needed to be gentle with myself and accept all parts of me. Afterall, self-respect and self-acceptance come with great accomplishment. It's a difficult process that can be made easier when someone embraces you wholeheartedly with loving compassion. Unfortunately, there are those who never receive the support and encouragement they require to move from the trauma they incurred in their youth to the healing and adjusting that should happen in adulthood.

CHAPTER 9

What Do You Want to Be Known For?

Grampy Butcher was my father's father. He pretended not to like it when Stephen and I called him "Grumpy Butcher." In fact, he pretended not to like any sound that came out of our mouths. At least I think he was pretending. He probably loved us kids in his own way. Every weekday afternoon at 4:00, he would tune his small black-and-white television to *The Great Money Movie*, which featured an old war film or something like *Planet of the Apes*. Eddie Driscoll would call fans of the show during commercial breaks to see if they could give him the secret word that flashed across the screen at some point during the movie. One ringy-dingy. Two ringy-dingies. Grampy was determined to win that jackpot. Then he would burp a "YUP!" as he got up from his wooden Boston rocker for supper after the show.

Since his parents were of Franco-Canadian descent, Grampy Butcher grew up speaking French. His father, who the family called Pere, carved oars for Old Town Canoe. His wife, Mere, was a naturalized citizen who never learned English, so she couldn't even talk to her own grandchildren who didn't know French. Grampy attended Catholic parochial elementary school in Orono, Maine, though I don't recall ever hearing about his education beyond that. I studied French in high school and was excited to talk with him in his native language, but he could only ever remember a word here and there. It had been a decade or two since his parents had died, so he couldn't recall the vocabulary.

Grampy Butcher was a World War II veteran. When he showed up to the recruiting office and the recruiters asked his name, he told them it was Antoine Boucher, but they informed him that his name henceforth would be an ordinary Anthony Butcher. He served as a paratrooper in the war. He wasn't allowed to reveal where he was stationed in his letters home, but like many other service members of the time, he wrote his location under the stamp on his letters to his sweetheart, who later became his wife. His military service changed him. There was an opportunity at one point for him and his brother to meet at a train station in Paris. The family story goes that they walked right past each other, not recognizing their own brother, until finally they figured it out and embraced on the station platform, happy to hug a loved one from home.

The war changed Grampy in other ways too. His short temper and sharp impatience were probably due to his time in the service. I've heard horror stories from other veterans about the demoralizing training they went through as well as the dehumanizing conditions under which they served. Later in his life, after his wife passed away, he filled his house with mass market paperbacks and VHS tapes of war stories, from fictional wartime dramas to historically accurate documentaries about the carnage and heartbreak of the era. It was like he was stuck in the trauma of his past, and he buried himself in it until his dying day.

Grampy could often be found weeding his garden or mowing the lawn in just his Dickey pants and black leather work boots, no shirt. In fact, he rarely ever wore a shirt, and when he did it was never buttoned up. His beer belly stuck out, and his chest hair was much like the hair on his head: gray, curly, and thick. He perpetually had a couple of day's growth of a scratchy beard and often smelled of stale body odor. Grampy had no teeth, but that didn't stop him from eating his pork chops or London broil almost every night.

Often sitting at the worn, dark-stained wood kitchen table opposite his wife, Grampy would strip the plastic coating off yards of reclaimed copper wire so he could sell it to the junkyard for cash. He also had this curious ritual of emptying his tobacco pipe by tapping it into the palm of his hand and then immediately turning his hand over to dump the spent tobacco onto the table. In real time it looked like a sleight-of-hand magic trick. Tap dump. Tap dump. Then he would press new tobacco into the bowl, strike a match to light it, and breathe the smoke deep into his lungs before scooping up the pile of ashes and walking it to the garbage can with his pipe held between his gums.

Grampy worked at the local textile mill. Every morning before dawn, Grammy Butcher would wake him up with a broomstick because, after years in the military, he had developed the habit of waking up swinging his fists, ready for a fight. Mill work was good, honest, hard work, but it came with hazards. For one thing, Grampy's fingernails were always black from getting caught in the machinery at the mill. It was common to watch him peel his crushed fingernails off at the kitchen table. As a young child, I wondered if I, too, would lose my fingernails when I grew up, as though it were part of the aging process. One of the perks of working at the mill was that Grampy had access to lots of tools. In 1970, he gave my mother, his new daughter-in-law, a pair of fabric shears with the name Marilyn scratched on the blade for a wedding gift. He told her not to worry because Marilyn would get some new scissors and everything would work out fine. It was his unique way of expressing his affection.

Plenty of family visited Grammy and Grampy Butcher in their modest home, so the living room often became rather crowded. When it was difficult to find a seat, anyone who walked into the room looking for someplace to sit would be met with Grampy and everyone—including us kids—extending our arms low and sticking our thumbs up. This was a crude joke that implied the standing person was welcome to sit on our thumbs if they were going to complain about the limited seating. It never occurred to me that this was inappropriate in any way. It was just the way things were done.

There was a ritual in Grammy and Grampy Butcher's house that the men would cook a particular dish for the family. I have no idea where he learned this recipe because we have no Pole blood in our line, but Grampy would make golumpkis. He would ceremoniously stuff and roll boiled cabbage leaves with hamburger, rice, onions, and peppers, then place each tender package into a large roasting pan, reverently layer them with sauerkraut, cover the pan, and cook them for what seemed like a very long time. This was the closest I ever saw my grandfather get to being religious. In all other spiritual matters, he forbade his family from going to any church because during the war he saw how badly the Catholic church conducted itself, aligning with the Nazis. He lost his faith and refused to let his wife and children be suckered by organized religion. In any case, the cabbage rolls were delicious with ketchup.

I sometimes wonder what Grampy's legacy is. What would he want to be known for? I suppose he would want to be recognized for the sacrifices he made to fight in the war, the time he spent away from his home and his family, and the training and missions that stripped away the innocence of his youth. I believe he would want to be known for his tireless work ethic, putting in years of his life at the mill and working on his house and his garden. I wonder whether he considered himself a family man or if his time serving as a soldier stripped him of his ability to attach to and connect with the people who were closest to him. Grampy was complicated, and my love for him was complex. His impatient shushing during his wartime TV shows is weighed against his loving preparation of a special meal for his family. We think he loved us, in his own peculiar way. Only he would know for sure.

His legacy for me is to remind me that life's experiences can be traumatic, and it can be easy to get stuck in the cycle of stimulus/response. Surviving from one trigger to the next while technically enduring the days and hours of life is not thriving. The recruiting office literally changed Grampy's identity, giving him a new name, and new haircut, and altering him so much that his own brother couldn't recognize him at that train station in Paris. The church had changed me, too, but I didn't need to accept those changes as permanent. I wanted more for my life and the lives of my children. They saw me crying many times throughout the years, and they understood that some days were "bed days" when I just needed to be alone with my depression and anxiety. I felt like an alien in my perfect life, and there were times when I had to remind myself not to wish this precious time away with my young family. I regret that the trauma of living a life I didn't feel I belonged in bled into my relationships with my children, but I didn't want this to be my legacy or their heritage. Fortunately for us all, a dear friend came to my rescue just in the nick of time.

Near the end of 2017, my friend Emma invited me to become one of her clients. She needed someone to practice on for her life coaching certification. Of course, being the polite friend I was, I accepted her invitation, and we got down to work. After taking tests to assess my strengths and interests, I was surprised to discover that creativity was a strength for me! She evaluated my personality dynamics using the Myers-Briggs Type Indicator, and we talked about goals from my youthful days and what progress I had made on them. Then she asked me the single question that changed my life: "What do you want to be known for?" This question made me dig deep into my psyche. Until that point, I had spent most of my adult life being a mother, but would that be my only legacy? Motherhood is noble. Hats off to any parent who undertakes child rearing in a thoughtful, deliberate way. But I thought back to when I was 17, before getting my patriarchal blessing. I knew I didn't feel called to have children, but what did I want instead?

I did the calculations and knew that my empty nest years were approaching, but I had a 17-year-old plan to end my life when my youngest graduated from high school, and that plan was still in effect. I asked myself whether suicide was what I wanted to be remembered for. I had never thought of it this way before, and the effect was jarring. I wanted my legacy to be something my family could be proud of, but I was on a collision course for serving up a hefty helping of shame to them for the rest of their lives. Did I want to teach my children that this was how they should resolve their problems? I began to see the fault in the logic of my plan and felt safe to reveal my situation to Emma.

"I have to be honest with you. You're wasting your time working with me. I don't plan to be around much longer, and so all these evaluations and assessments are of no use."

The busy coffee shop where we met was dim and trendy. Ambient lighting met with ambient music to create an atmosphere of buzzing productivity as fellow customers and coffee drinkers tapped away on their laptops. The fragrance of roasting coffee beans, though stark upon first entering the shop, became an ambient smell after a while of sitting in our regular corner seats with leather chairs and a low, wooden table. Emma focused her direct attention and stern eyebrows on my face and asked, "What do you mean you don't plan to be around much longer?"

I described the details of my 17-year plan to complete raising my children and then close the book on my life.

Rather than overreacting, she replied with empathy and compassion: "How do you feel about writing a few more chapters in your life that include some happiness and hope?"

We held candid conversations about my worth in this life and my potential for a future I never dared to dream of. She nurtured my timid self-esteem and encouraged me with love and acceptance. Her methods were kind and supportive, and I began to see a life for myself beyond that of mother. The church had taught me that motherhood was my greatest achievement and the fulfillment of my eternal purpose, but what came next? Was I just supposed to wait around until my children started having children of their own so that I could be a grandmother? Again, a noble calling, but not the right aspiration for me.

I realized that I had been living a very small life and trying to make myself small in everything I did—a habit I picked up in my childhood being raised by adult children of alcoholics. I tried not to make too much noise. I tried not to take up too much space. I tried not to do anything that would annoy the people I lived with so that they would be able to tolerate me and we could have peace in our home. But my life wasn't peaceful inside. I was constantly checking to see if I was talking too much, leaving my belongings out in the common areas of the house, or making too much of a mess. I was making sure not to do so many things that my list of things I did feel comfortable doing was minuscule and inauthentic. I could relate with the state of Grampy Butcher's house near the end of his life, with stacks of books and movies cluttering his living space, choking out his life force, and preventing him from inviting anyone into his home or his heart. His life became small as he buried himself alive with memorabilia and nostalgic reminders of his stolen youth and traumatic burden of wartime memories.

My life and my purpose needed to be bigger. I had more to offer the world, I just needed help from Emma to discover what that was and how to unleash it. After I surprisingly discovered that I was a creative soul in the assessments she gave me, Emma asked me if I had a dream career. It took a long time to uncover it, but eventually I recognized that I wanted to be a writer. I wanted to create art using words and imagination, so I set out to hone my professional skills and awaken my analytical brain.

I enrolled in business classes at the local state college and began applying myself toward a degree that would help me build a career. Later I decided to switch back to an English degree since that was where most of my credits were from during my past college experience, thus expediting my graduation progress. School opened my mind to grander ideas about life and living. A philosophy professor changed the course of my life when she asked us to write an essay. I chose to submit a personal narrative about my time as a closeted lesbian in the Mormon church for nearly four decades. Writing my thoughts on the subject brought me clarity and understanding.

A rewrite of that essay would later be published in an anthology called "I Spoke to You with Silence," by the *University of Utah Press.*

As my realizations progressed, I began recognizing that the path to my future couldn't be walked with a husband by my side, which was both devastating and liberating. How many changes could I make if I weren't married anymore? I could move to my home state of Maine, which had been calling me back for years. I could live an open and honest identity as a lesbian. I could make decisions on my own and not have to worry about anyone else's opinions about my choices. But I didn't want to break my husband's heart. He was a nice man who deserved an intact family and a life partner who would approach retirement years with him. However, I had spent the last 17 years dying in a life I was living for other people. It was time to begin living for myself. I made my decision, choosing life over the darkness of planning my death. Emma deserves the credit for saving my life and pointing me in a hopeful direction for a future full of possibilities.

I felt like a beach ball that had been forced deep underwater for a long time and was now being released along with the burden it had been under for years. This feeling shot up into the air in jubilant celebration. Just as the war had changed Grampy, the church had changed me, but unlike him, I would no longer be stuck in the trauma of my past. I had a larger life to live. Now the trick was to discover where it would take me. I had to dig deep and determine whether I had the courage to make the changes that needed to be made.

CHAPTER 10

Courage to Change

Second grade was a pivotal time for me. Our family moved from one side of Bangor to the other, my parents' marriage was deteriorating into resentment and arguments, and I was attending a new school and experiencing all the hope-filled and fearful feelings that come with that. I made friends in the neighborhood with whom I played kickball and whiffle ball in the empty lot next door. I climbed trees and I skinned knees. I stole the neighbor's overgrown rhubarb, dipping it in a bowl of sugar for a sweet and tart treat. I climbed another neighbor's retaining wall built out of railroad ties. On rainy days, I put my bathing suit on and danced in the puddles. I built a clubhouse out of scrap wood and old blankets, rode my bike to the park where I played Frisbee golf, and ran around barefoot. I played outside until the sun went down and the streetlights came on. This is also the year I met Mrs. Sweeny.

Such a young, gentle, and playful soul, Mrs. Sweeny was my second-grade teacher. Her build was slight, and she had a great tan that she either worked on regularly or inherited from her ancestors. She had short wavy hair and the kindest eyes, and she habitually showed compassion for the mini humans around her. She gave out peanuts in the shell as rewards for good performance and behavior. Of course we had the option to eat the salty nuts, shell and all; however, if we exercised a little self-restraint, we could use the peanuts as currency to bid on items for recess. Indoor recess days were my favorite because I liked to purchase either the Pink Panther jigsaw puzzle or the record player that played the song "You Can't Roller Skate in a Buffalo Herd." Outdoor recess was fun too. I remember a jump rope and a kickball being offered in the daily recess auction.

One fateful outdoor recess day, Mrs. Sweeny looked out her window and saw me hiding near the classroom door, crying under my yellow raincoat hood. She opened the door and invited me inside. Before she even asked me what was wrong, she encouraged me to blow my nose and get a drink of water. After calming down and feeling like I was in a safe space, I confided in her that the kids were making fun of me for my new haircut. Until that day, I had long brown hair with blunt full bangs. The hairstyle became difficult to manage on a daily basis, so my mother cut my hair. I loved the new look and felt so proud and happy to show it off at school. But kids are cruel and make fun of anything different or new, so my happy day didn't stay joyful for long. Mrs. Sweeny gave me a long hug and allowed me to stay inside for the rest of recess. Her words comforted me, and when I asked her if I could keep my hood up during the remainder of the school day, she compassionately agreed.

So many aspects of my world were changing. I felt the pressure of being the new kid in school, and I maneuvered through all the social hoops that must be jumped through when you're seven and an outsider. With my parents ending each day with loud arguments and vicious accusations, I had upheaval in my home life. I also noticed that I was different from the girly girls who played with dolls and wore lip gloss. My curiosity about bodies and sex was taking an unexpected turn as I had developed a crush on a girl at my old school. My life was in flux in so many ways, and although my power was limited,

I unwittingly navigated the best possible outcome for my haircut drama. The next day I felt more confident and somehow convinced the other students that my haircut was cool. They followed my lead and left me alone.

Mrs. Sweeny sent me the message that I could face the odds and win. She somehow taught me that I had the power to make my circumstances better and that I didn't have to settle for what the world dealt me. She gave me the courage to change, to improve, to grow, and this courage would serve me well in the future.

The summer after my school year with Mrs. Sweeny, I discovered that we were neighbors. I saw her out in her yard as I passed by her house, and I invited myself over, as only a child can. She invited me in for lemonade and cookies, and we had a nice chat about my math workbook, which I was still using even though it was summer. Her tidy home was covered in floral prints from her couch to the curtains, and it smelled like lilacs and Pledge. She was her usual cheerful self, but the juxtaposition of my teacher having a house instead of just sleeping at the school was too much for me. After that day we simply waved to each other instead of having formal visits, but she remains one of the most influential people in my young life. Her faith in me and my ability to change the things in my world that no longer serve me well has carried me through many difficult times and brought me to the summit of life changes, which was to leave the church, my family, and my home in search of a better life.

On the morning of August 3, 2020, I said goodbye to my family. My older son was awake and gave me a big hug and wished me well. Rune was still in bed, but I woke them up to say bye. Gary tried to escape to the shower, but I caught him in time and gave him a final hug standing under the dim hallway light outside the bathroom door. I got in my car, and with the help of my cousin Drago, we drove away from my home in Connecticut with a U-Haul full of my belongings and headed to Portland, Maine. I consider this date to be my New Life Day, and I will celebrate it every year for the rest of my life—for it is the day I chose life over death. I recalled Mrs. Sweeny's encouragement, and I mustered the courage to change my life for the better. Driving away from my home and family was very difficult. I was leaving behind so many memories in that house and so many memories with those loved ones with whom I had shared my life. I felt lonely but not desperate. I felt confident but not relieved. The excitement of the adventure soon took hold, and the relocation went without any trouble.

I settled into life quickly. Though I met my neighbors, all I could see of their faces was their eyes because these were COVID-19 times and we were all wearing masks to prevent the spread of disease. I was once again the new kid in the neighborhood, but I had the skills to make friends easily and was met with a warm welcome in my home state of Maine. I explored my new city with all the art, music, food, and beauty it had to offer. I took long walks from the ocean-front parks to the old cobblestoned parts of town. The city was so vibrant and alive, which fit my mood perfectly.

Discovering that I was thrilled to live alone, I filled all the rooms of my new rental apartment with furniture that I loved and decor that made me smile. My favorite design element was a wall of '80s album covers I printed out and placed in a grid above my couch in the living room. It coaxed a smile out of me every time I looked at it, and it was quite a conversation piece when I had guests. Living alone meant I could take up as much space as I wanted, which was a new experience for me. I had come from a childhood home where walking on eggshells was expected, then moved into a college apartment with roommates who I didn't want to annoy, then ultimately occupied a home with my husband and children where, although I was free to take up space, I was reluctant to do so out of habit and the fear of upsetting anyone.

In the greater Portland area, I met people from the queer community who showered me with acceptance and support. Ironically, I met my new best friends through a church. Although I wasn't prepared to attend church meetings yet, I was welcomed into a care group with a local congregation of the United Church of Christ, with whom I was connected through friends of friends when I still lived in Danbury. I've since learned that the queer community is great at connecting people who have similar needs or interests. I was introduced to this lovely group of individuals during the brief few months between my coming out to my family and my leaving Connecticut to start a new life. I was thrilled to get to know these queer church ladies and men through video calls ahead of my big move to Maine. This made my transition that much smoother because I didn't have to worry about winning them over or convincing them that my haircut was cool. As one of them affectionately remarked after my move, it takes a village to extricate a Mormon. These people became instant family.

Two of these amazing individuals were Vicky and Gloria, who swiftly took me under their wing and included me in their bubble of people they considered safe during the pandemic. We spent many lovely evenings playing cribbage, eating delicious food, and listening to LPs on their turntable. I learned more than I ever thought I would about the birds that frequented their feeders, and their cats were unusually welcoming to a stranger like me.

One of the best days of my life was the day Vicky and Gloria exchanged their wedding vows. It was a whole weekend affair, with very few guests, and I was incredibly honored to be one of them. The ceremony was beautifully simple and especially meaningful to them in so many ways. It was held outside on a beautiful August day. The dappled sunlight shone through the leaves of the large tree above their heads, and a handmade family heirloom rug supported their feet. The few friends and family gathered in a semicircle around these women, passing around the wedding rings while each guest shared well-wishes and blessings for them and their union. My heart grew three sizes that day, just like the Grinch. My broken heart healed in a manner that I didn't expect. Fed by the love that these two women had for each other, I was proud to be a lesbian, a woman, and a person of limited but budding faith. My eyes were opened to newly possible levels of commitment and love. It was a beautiful start to my healing.

One of the most significant parts of this day was when Vicky and Gloria asked me if I would sign my name as a witness of their union on their marriage certificate. When I got married in Utah in 1996, there wasn't even an option for a woman to be a witness on an official government document. Participating in administrative affairs wasn't a woman's place in the church. Although Gloria and Vicky's invitation confused me at first, I accepted with enthusiasm. I signed that legal document in ink, but I felt like I was signing it in the blood, sweat, and tears of so many years of oppression and misogynistic overbearance. The experience moved me. I was honored and humbled. I understood that everything about their wedding was meticulously planned, and I took seriously their charge to witness their wedding ceremony, their love, and the beginning of their new life together as a married couple.

It takes courage to change. It takes support from mentors and friends. It takes fortitude and endurance, but what it gives back in return is precious and dear. Self-respect blossoms, confidence booms, life improves. It gets better. It gets better. It gets better.

CHAPTER 11

The End of a Cold, Dark Night

Halloween always belonged to our father when we were young. He loved to drive us to the neighboring town where he grew up and show us off to his old friends and neighbors. Mum would lovingly bundle Stephen and I up for the cold and do her best to fit our costumes over our snowsuits. Some years we had homemade outfits that Mum made, like a clown or a samurai warrior. Other years we wore the swishy plastic store-bought costumes from the '70s, the ones with the masks that had impossibly small holes for our eyes and mouths. The only constant was the cold weather.

We would shiver down the paved roads of Veazie's village in search of candy, with Dad directing us to the houses that were safe for goody grabbing and us taking turns ringing doorbells or knocking on aluminum storm doors. Invariably, the little old ladies would open the door a crack and ask if we were from the neighborhood. Then my dad would step into the circle of porch light and announce who we were. Only after they recognized him would they give us each a single piece of candy or an apple, and then they would want to catch up for a minute while our enthusiasm cooled off—and our toes froze. But damn it, every year that apple always rotted in the bag before I finished my candy.

Our annual trick-or-treat nights ended at Aunt Maude's house. She served homemade donuts and hot apple cider, and as we sat in her parlor, we thawed and progressively removed articles of outerwear clothing. Mittens first, then hats and scarfs; unzip this, untie that, while our chocolate-filled candy bags melted from the heat of her wood stove. We savored the crunchy sugar and cinnamon that coated her cider donuts. We held the hot ceramic mugs under our chins to feel the steam on our faces and inhale the seasonal fragrance of mulling spices. Aunt Maude faithfully caught us up on all the family gossip for the year and, undoubtedly, collected more gossip from us to share with others. She was my Grammy Butcher's aunt, which made her prehistoric to us. Her crepey neck skin bounced up and down when she laughed, and her clear, piercing blue eyes looked directly into our souls when she spoke to us. She was a good egg, as Dad would say, and she was a safe haven after a long, cold, dark night. Sometimes cold, dark nights can lead you to unusual places for healing and closure.

If you had told me even a year before that I would consult an expert in shamanic healing to resolve my religious trauma, I wouldn't have believed you. I was still bruised from feeling like I had been beaten with the Jesus hammer for nearly four decades. Friends encouraged me to attend church services soon after arriving in Maine, but I explained my reticence in a colorful way: you can lead a horse to water, but before you push him in, think how a wet horse smells. I wasn't ready.

Almost a year after moving to Maine and working with a therapist, I resumed reading books about spirituality, and it sparked something in me. I was still traumatized about churches, but I came into acquaintance with a Unitarian Universalist minister.

Her personality was peaceful and spiritually mature, so I turned to her for advice on how to heal and how to reclaim my spirituality. In her wisdom, she recognized that my healing was beyond her skill expertise, so she referred me to a shaman friend named Sarah who used Native healing techniques.

Since this was during COVID-19 times, our session was conducted over Zoom. Sarah and I discussed what she would do to invite her healing sources to help me. Though I was a little skeptical, I was willing to believe because I was tired of feeling so lost and hurt. In preparation for our session, I had sent her my essay about my experiences in the church and the trauma I incurred there. As she began our ceremony, she lit a candle while chanting. She paid respect to the four main directions on the compass before blindfolding herself and pulling out her drum. I added my faith to her drumming sounds, hoping for healing, preparing myself to receive whatever kind of message she had for me, and opening myself up to the possibility that she had access to something that could help. The drumming stopped. She removed her blindfold.

"I understand that you're here for religious trauma," Sarah paused dramatically, "but first we need to rescue your brother."

Stephen had been gone for 17 years, and in all that time I had never felt his presence—or even felt assured that he continued to exist. This suggestion that he needed rescuing shocked me, but I was willing to hear what Sarah had to say.

"Your brother is in a hell of his own making. He believes he needs to suffer because of what he was taught at church."

Stephen had always been haunted by what he called his demons. I never asked him specifically what those demons were, but I assumed he suffered from depression the way I did. He self-medicated with drugs and alcohol to an unhealthy extent for the second half of his short 30-year life, and this turned him into someone he wasn't. And now, here was Sarah telling me he was punishing himself for his choices because of the lessons he got from the church when he was a teen. My heart broke for him. Whatever representation Sarah had of him was in pain. She described his prison as "dark, small, and anguishing," so I was all for helping release him from it. She used her sources to open his prison wall, but before he left his torture, he simply conveyed the word "FORGIVENESS." I could only assume his burden of guilt was from the poor choices he made in his life. I granted my forgiveness wholeheartedly and asked for his forgiveness as well, through my tears. For the first time since his death, I felt him close. I felt his pain. I felt his love.

Shaman Sarah guided him to a peaceful place full of light and love. I didn't know how much of this to believe, but it brought me peace to hear that he was released from his self-imposed prison and that I had a chance to communicate my feelings of love and forgiveness to him. Sarah closed that vision and turned her attention to me.

"Now, let's see what we can do to help you." She started drumming and chanting while I pulled myself back together, physically and emotionally. "Since your baptism is the moment you lost your power, we will focus on that day first and untie the spiritual knots your soul is in."

She described the scene in her mind of untying knots and the threads falling to the floor. She struggled to resolve the pain of my trauma coming up through the years, so I divulged that I lost my power again when I went to the temple for the first time at age 21. I explained that I was expected to make promises to the church and to God about obedience and faithfulness, that in return I was promised eternal life in the highest degree of Heaven, and that I would be blessed to live forever with my family members who were also faithful and obedient to the church. But if I didn't live up to these promises, I told her, I would be damned. I made these previously undisclosed covenants under social pressure since I was in a room full of members of my home congregation, including my mother who was sitting right next to me. Knowing she loved me and that it was her deepest desire to live with me forever in Heaven, I bowed my head and said yes to the covenants. From that moment on, I told Sarah, my life was not my own. Everything I did, said, and thought was only to fulfill that promise of obedience and faithfulness to God.

Eventually, Shaman Sarah broke through the knots and released me from the bonds that had been holding me down for so long. Describing the scene in her vision, she told me the threads from those spiritual knots were now on the floor around me.

"Is there any significance of a black bear in your life?" she asked. "Is there anyone who could be represented by this big black bear I'm seeing?" It only took me a minute to recognize Grammy Sullivan as the big mama bear that she always was for me. "The bear is eating up the threads that lay around you. And she has a message for you, 'Don't let anyone do this to you again!'" That was Grammy, alright! She had shown up to rescue me, to relieve me from my pain and the damage that the church had done to my soul. Having felt close to Grammy many times in my life after her passing, I could recognize her spiritual signature. Thank you, Grammy. I love you.

When her vision was over, Sarah thanked me for allowing her to be part of my healing. She said it was a distinct honor and privilege to witness the work we had done together. Once again, I didn't know how much of the healing session to believe in, but it honestly made me feel better, and I did achieve the healing that I was hoping for. I can't explain it, but ever since that shamanic healing session, my heart has been healed. I'm whole in a way I've never been before. Sarah restored my faith and my capacity to believe and feel. She was a good egg, and she was a safe haven after a long, cold, dark night of the soul.

CHAPTER 12

I Am Resilient

The word *resilient* connotes bravery that snaps back, wash after wash. I am resilient like the palm trees in tropical locales, which bend with the wind instead of being uprooted by the tumult. My bravery in the face of change and loss shows me how resilient I am. It shows me the depths of my character and the commitment I have to my future happiness and success.

Look at what I did!

- I left the Church of Jesus Christ of Latter-day Saints after 38 years of faithful devotion, as a result of extensive study and agonizing soul searching. I read books and listened to speakers about spirituality outside the confines of my own religion and found that there was more to spirituality than just obedience and loyalty.

- I came out as a lesbian to my husband, my children, and my extended family, risking scrutiny and exclusion. I knew full well that my friends and family in the church wouldn't be able to support me because of my association with the queer community, yet it was important enough for me to allow my loved ones into my new life of truth and authenticity. Surprisingly, I've received many private expressions of love and acceptance from these folks, which have warmed my heart and restored my faith in humanity.

- I drove a U-Haul away from my family and our home in pursuit of my own happiness and fulfillment. For the first time in my life, I followed through with a commitment I made to be true and faithful to myself. Leaving my old life was an act of faith in myself and an expression of faith in an autonomous future.

- I thwarted my own 17-year-old suicide plan and instead created a new existence filled with hope and possibility. I traveled from the very depths of despair, scraping the bottom of my existence in search of acceptance, to the unfettered exhilaration of choosing life over choosing death.

- I moved back to Maine. I came home to rediscover my roots and connect with others who share my ideals and values. Portland, Maine, is a relatively safe place for a lesbian to live her life openly and proudly. I became reacquainted with high school friends who showed unwavering love and support. Their friendship means the world to me, and I missed it since leaving the state soon after graduation.

- I returned to school and recommitted to an education that will help me build a fulfilling and profitable career. There's nothing like the air of possibility that can be felt on a college campus. It's contagious and exhilarating. I fill my lungs with it in every inhale and expel my old air of doubt and uncertainty. I am resilient. I am smart. I am successful.

- I stood up to patriarchal authority figures who oppressed me in the past. In the moment I called my bishop a prick, I claimed myself. I staked my claim on my own life and my own choices.

In that moment, my life changed for the better, as did the life of my trans child.

- I gave myself permission to be autonomous, and I gained self-respect through my resilient words and actions of empowerment. I am enough. I am plenty. I am a handful, no doubt, but I am a human who has finally joined the human race instead of thinking of myself as elite and above everyone and everything. I welcome myself to the world and all the joy it has to offer.

I am resilient. I am fucking resilient! And you can be, too. There's a courageous beast inside you, and it's waiting to be given permission to wreak havoc on your behalf. There's hope and possibility in your heart. You are only as stuck as you believe you are. Have faith in yourself. Talk kindly to yourself. Be your own best cheerleader and fill your quick access contacts list with people who love you and want you to succeed. Don't let fear drive your bus. There are experiences from your life that can give you the strength to stand up to authority and break the cycle of oppression. Draw on the courage of others until you find it with yourself. Reach out for help to find your purpose and your mission, and keep reaching out until you find what you need. The good news is that love wins. Love yourself enough to try making these changes. You are worthy. You, my friend, are resilient. Prove it to yourself today.

Conclusion

I just signed my divorce agreement in front of a notary public. So many emotions are surging through my mind. I know ending the marriage is the right thing to do for me. I sacrificed over 20 years of my life for my family to provide a stable home for my children. I tried to spare my ex-husband from the hurt that has inevitably come between us. Even though I wasn't a perfect mother during those years, I honestly tried my best every single day. And now that I'm at the crossroads of married and not married, I find more ambivalence than I expected. My heart is torn between who I was for so many years and who I have become over the last couple of years since coming out in January of 2020. Divorce is the obvious right path for me, as a lesbian who was married to a man. However, I'm not used to making decisions that hurt those I love the most. I'm forever breaking up the only nuclear family my children have known. For the first time in my life, I'm acting in my own best interest at the expense of my loved ones.

On the brighter side, I've mended my relationship with my mother. In an effort to reestablish our friendship, she and I have practiced either genuine forgetfulness or selective amnesia. When I came out to her in January of 2020, she told me she loved me very much but that she couldn't support me. I understand her predicament. As a member of the LDS church, she isn't permitted to sympathize with members of the queer community. So I meet her where she is. We don't talk much about it. We just get together every couple of months and watch movies, play cribbage, and cook delicious food. Honestly, she was more upset that I might be a Democrat than she was about my being gay and leaving the church.

To my delight, I've maintained strong relationships with my adult children. We FaceTime every week and keep each other updated with current events in our lives. We express love and concern, and we're building our relationships stronger with every phone call and visit. My oldest is getting engaged and will soon be married in the temple. This is a ceremony that I'm no longer allowed to attend, and I'll miss the event because I don't believe what the church teaches. But can I blame him for wanting to be married in the building that I taught him was the most sacred place on Earth? A place that's so special that only the most faithful members of the church can enter? So I'll wait patiently outside on the manicured grounds of the temple building, for him and his new bride to present themselves to the world as a newly married couple. There will be tears, but there will be no regrets on my part.

I've also found romantic love. I have found a person with whom I can be authentic and sincere. My life is enriched by her nurturing presence, and she doesn't just appreciate what I can do for her or what perfect image I can project of us. She loves me for who I am. She loves *me*. And I'm emphatically in love with her.

I know in my heart and soul that I am worthy of love. I am worthy of a life filled with hope and possibility, worthy of a life worth living.

Book Group Discussion Questions

1. What sources do you credit for your spiritual beliefs? How did you confirm or discard them as you grew into maturity?

2. What significant person influenced you most in your youth? In which ways did they help you grow and learn about the world? Have you had the opportunity to mentor someone?

3. What have your experiences been with the LGBTQIA+ community? How have those interactions changed with increased representation and exposure?

4. When was a time you bowed to authority figures rather than following your own intuition? What were the benefits of this decision, and what were the detriments?

5. How has mental health affected you or your loved ones? Have you found treatment to be effective? How would you contribute to the conversation about mental health services in our current climate?

6. What steps have you taken in the past to conform to societal expectations? Describe any pressures from loved ones or associates to be something less than your authentic self.

7. What would you like your legacy to be? Are your current life choices in alignment with that?

8. What changes has this discussion prompted you to make? How will this book influence the way you move in the world?

Acknowledgements

This work is only possible because of the love and support of so many amazing people.

Thank you to Julia Cameron, who inspired me to tap into my creativity and develop the habit of writing down my thoughts and ideas in her book *The Artist's Way*.

Thank you to Alanna and the Triangle Community Center in Norwalk, Connecticut, for receiving me with open arms when I came out and for being the first to include me in the queer community.

Thank you to my dear friends in my book club in Stamford, Connecticut. I have never met another group of women with bigger hearts or bigger smiles.

Their love and acceptance have inspired and encouraged me at every step.

Thank you to my LGBTQIA+ care group at the UCC in Portland, Maine, for wrapping their arms around me in my hour of need. They made my journey easier and my burden lighter.

Thank you to Judy for showing me genuine Christian love and for restoring my hope in the Divine, whatever form that takes.

Thank you to Jenn, Bailly, and Brandi at Publish Your Purpose for supporting me throughout the writing and publishing process. They are all short and mighty women who are changing the world with their gifts and talents. I appreciate their mission to amplify marginalized voices.

Thank you to Nancy Graham-Tillman for improving my writing with her gentle correction and her fierce encouragement. This book is better because of her expertise.

Thank you to Giada for encouraging me to write my story and for teaching me that philosophy lives and breathes in everything we study.

Thank you to Christine for teaching me the difference between surviving and truly living.

Thank you to Kerry Spencer Pray and the Queer Mormon Women Project for fostering opportunities to share thoughts and express ideas about how to heal and how to move forward.

Thank you to Nicole for our weekly check-ins. Her encouragement and advice have elevated me as a writer and as a human.

Thank you to the Mama Dragons for their support of parents with queer children. The stories they share are both heartbreaking and heartwarming. Keep going, Mamas! You're doing important work.

Thank you to Mary and Shelly of the Latter Day Lesbian Podcast for helping me laugh and cry my way to a place of healing and acceptance.

Thank you to Heather Vickery for hosting me on her podcast and helping me make professional connections. Her mission is inspiring, and her enthusiasm is contagious.

Thank you to Glennon Doyle and Abby Wambach for teaching me that I can do hard things, and for reminding me that I am a goddamned cheetah!

And a huge sincere thanks to the many friends and associates who have reviewed this text and contributed valuable feedback toward the success of my project.

About the Author

Chris Davis was a lifelong devout Mormon who checked all the expected boxes of wife, mother, teacher, leader, follower, and believer until 2020 when she left her family and her church to fulfill her own personal destiny as a gay woman and independent thinker. She remains close with her two adult children, one of whom is a believing member of the church and the other who is a transgender man who has also left the church.

Chris's other works include contributing an essay about her experience of being queer in the LDS church in an anthology called *I Spoke to You with Silence,* published in 2022 by the *University of Utah Press.* She lives quite happily in her home state of Maine.

You can connect with Chris and explore other podcasts and public appearances on her website: ChrisDavisProud.com.

The B Corp Movement

Dear reader,

Thank you for reading this book and joining the Publish Your Purpose community! You are joining a special group of people who aim to make the world a better place.

What's Publish Your Purpose About?
Our mission is to elevate the voices often excluded from traditional publishing. We intentionally seek out authors and storytellers with diverse backgrounds, life experiences, and unique perspectives to publish books that will make an impact in the world.

Certified

Corporation

Beyond our books, we are focused on tangible, action-based change. As a woman- and LGBTQ+-owned company, we are committed to reducing inequality, lowering levels of poverty, creating a healthier environment, building stronger communities, and creating high-quality jobs with dignity and purpose.

As a Certified B Corporation, we use business as a force for good. We join a community of mission-driven companies building a more equitable, inclusive, and sustainable global economy. B Corporations must meet high standards of transparency, social and environmental performance, and accountability as determined by the nonprofit B Lab. The certification process is rigorous and ongoing (with a recertification requirement every three years).

How Do We Do This?
We intentionally partner with socially and economically disadvantaged businesses that meet our sustainability goals. We embrace and encourage our authors and employee's differences in race, age, color, disability, ethnicity, family or marital status, gender identity or expression, language, national origin, physical and mental ability, political affiliation, religion, sexual orientation, socio-economic status, veteran status, and other characteristics that make them unique.

Community is at the heart of everything we do—from our writing and publishing programs to contributing to social enterprise nonprofits like reSET (https://www.resetco.org/) and our work in founding B Local Connecticut.

We are endlessly grateful to our authors, readers, and local community for being the driving force behind the equitable and sustainable world we are building together.

To connect with us online, or publish with us,
visit us at www.publishyourpurpose.com.

Elevating Your Voice,

Jenn T Grace

Jenn T. Grace
Founder, Publish Your Purpose

www.ingramcontent.com/pod-product-compliance
Lightning Source LLC
Chambersburg PA
CBHW020451130626
46549CB00001B/376